Winter Wonderland

Winter Delights

Edited By Roseanna Caswell

First published in Great Britain in 2024 by:

Young Writers
Remus House
Coltsfoot Drive
Peterborough
PE2 9BF
Telephone: 01733 890066
Website: www.youngwriters.co.uk

All Rights Reserved
Book Design by Ashley Janson
© Copyright Contributors 2024
Softback ISBN 978-1-83565-422-4
Printed and bound in the UK by BookPrintingUK
Website: www.bookprintinguk.com
YB0590CZ

Foreword

Dear Reader,

Welcome to Winter Wonderland, a showcase for our nation's most brilliant young poets to share their thoughts and feelings during the coldest months of the year. This collection covers every aspect of wintertime alongside deeper explorations of emotions and the topics that are important to them.

Young Writers was established in 1991 to nurture creativity in our children and young adults, to give them an interest in poetry and an outlet to express themselves. Seeing their work in print will encourage them to keep writing as they grow and become our poets of tomorrow.

Selecting the poems has been challenging and immensely rewarding. The effort and imagination invested by these young writers makes their poems a pleasure to enjoy reading time and time again. I hope you enjoy reading them as much as we did.

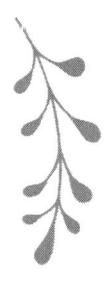

Contents

Independent Entrants

Priscilla-Grace Aina (14)	1
Liv Baker (16)	2
Anabella Calfa (12)	8
Phoebe Wilson (10)	11
Fatima Hussain (12)	12
Ren Owen (13)	15
Sam Singh (11)	16
Danny Sokolov (11)	19
Hetvi Patel (15)	20
Amelia Grala (13)	22
Khloe Ndjoli (14)	25
Mary Eunice Oderanti (12)	26
Manpreet Kaur Singh (14)	29
Benjamin Doeteh (17)	30
Emma Mareva (13)	32
Bella Viney (13)	34
Aleena Hussain (11)	36
Chessie Young (14)	38
Ronit Gupta (12)	40
Khadija Hingorani (11)	42
Jaye Sayagh (14)	44
Jasmine Koc (11)	46
Heidi Gottschall (12)	48
Umaymah Hussain (10)	51
Phoebe Allen (17)	52
Imose Osarhiemen (11)	54
Chloe Russell (15)	56
Aurelia Littlejohn (15)	58
Paige Munn (9)	60
Maria Ivescu (12)	62
Maria Miah (11)	64
Harley Morris (13)	66
Eisha Tajammal (18)	68
Alice Talbot (10)	70
Danielle Erikume (10)	72
Isabelle Poulton (12)	74
Amie Varley (14)	76
Mackenzie Shurmer (14)	78
Safia Ali (17)	80
Het Patel (8)	82
Isabelle Trilloe (15)	84
Athena Campbell (14)	86
Rida Jaffery (14)	88
Nishtha Ghelani (13)	90
Gracie Allen (14)	92
Livie Johnston (14)	94
Siddhant Gupta (13)	96
Hanna Elkaram (18)	98
Abira Loganathan (11)	100
Bobby Dearing (11)	102
Pia Patel (13)	104
Nadia Sysak (13)	106
Daniel Irfan (9)	108
Akshayan Vivekanantharajah (7)	110
Thomas Cassidy (8)	112
Adetomi Adeyemi (11)	114
Maggie-May Prior (15)	116
Ivaanya Marwah (12)	118
Aden Fincken (15)	120
Grey Mazillius (14)	122
Gurvir Sandhu (12)	124
Piper Jayne Lewis (13)	126
Layla Saunders (9)	128
Alanis Harrison (11)	130
Laiba Sohail (14)	132
Sarah Ward (11)	134
Summer Petch (14)	136
Cali Hughes (18)	138
Ayat Waseem Khan (8)	140

Name	Page
Taifa Rawza (12)	142
Scarlet Carr (11)	144
Gabriella Rundle-Shahzad (16)	145
Shrinjal Mishra (9)	146
Oliver Champney (11)	147
Victoria Cicha (16)	148
Amelia Barnes (13)	149
Yasmin Abdullah (11)	150
Holly Pitts (12)	152
Tanaka Natalie Gundani (14)	153
Skylar Jolly (11)	154
Bella Lane (14)	156
Param Ghelani (7)	157
Mansa Tahir (9)	158
Anastazja Clark (9)	159
Lily Marsden-Mellin (11)	160
Syeda Bisma (13)	161
Mathey Dezhev (11)	162
Claudia Muller (12)	163
Syeda Anisa Mumtaz Nakvi (10)	164
Toby Taylor (16)	166
Mia Flowerday (10)	168
Gregori Masliakovas (9)	170
Sara Abdussalam (16)	171
Esther Mbogol (10)	172
Aadita Keshari (7)	174
Ayesha Siddiqah Ahmed (16)	175
Olivia Rose Blake (11)	176
Azka Bhatti (13)	178
Prithviraj Chauhan (11)	179
Alex-Kate Phillips-Hawkes (16)	180
Gisele Yang (9)	181
Niamh Bacon-Breen (12)	182
Oshmi Jayakody (11)	184
Alysha Dosanjh (12)	185
Tamara Kramer (14)	186
Purity Ihesie (10)	187
Charmaine Mak (9)	188
Daisy Adela Anderson (12)	190
Ellie Bartles-Smith (13)	192
Halimah Al-Aswad (11)	194
Amy Stevenson (12)	195
Dewi Miles (12)	196
Olivia Henry (11)	198
Olivia McGregor (16)	199
Marley Prot-Lane (15)	200
Yusuf A Husny (11)	201
Lily Turner (8)	202
Mawulolo Koliasa (10)	203
Eleanor Lancaster (14)	204
Lara Johnston (9)	206
Mason James (7)	207
Amandeep Bhakar (10)	208
Holly Hopkinson (14)	210
Natalia Winiarska (9)	211
Poppy Orr (17)	212
Harley Johnson (6)	213
Zikoranaudodimma Iyayi (8)	214
Aizah Nadeem (10)	215
Ali Fareed (11)	216
Betty Rogers (9)	217
Owen Taylor (12)	218
Ameerah Ghariani (16)	219
Imogen Gannon (12)	220
Kacey Compton (13)	221
Anaya Hassan (11)	222
Samantha Hull (7)	223
Sancheka Sreeharan (11)	224
Precious Onuoha (10)	225
Paige Polley (9)	226
Meerab Sheikh (13)	227
Tyler James Forth (16)	228
Nathania Chimduwem (8)	230
Umaima Mukhtar Zia (13)	231
Sophie Goodier (11)	232
Haiqa Aziz (9)	233
Keelan Stringer (9)	234
Victoria Anyaegbu (9)	235
Ella Koc (8)	236
Isabella Howes-Warnes (10)	237
Amaoge Okoli (15)	238
Rifky Izaak (15)	239
Kabiven Vivekanantharajah (11)	240
Adele Amour (10)	241
Catherine Holmes (9)	242
Kadie Rasmussen (16)	243

Ashleen Khela (11)	244
Arabella Pasquariello (9)	245
E R Harper (16)	246
Noelle Ngan (7)	247
Samuel Kiwanuka-Musoke (7)	248
Amrit Singh Pannu (8)	249
Ariana Jones (8)	250
Blossom Huntington (8)	251
Mia Spilsbury (8)	252
Chloe Griffiths (12)	253
Esha Raheel (10)	254
Charlie Page (13)	255
Chester Steele (7)	256
Daisy Corbet (12)	257
Sayara Munasinghe (5)	258
Dhruvi Patel (9)	259
Carly-Jade Sharman (12)	260
Logan Esposito Dotchin (7)	261
Mia Drummond (9)	262
Janiru Kudahetty (9)	263

The Poems

Winter

Winter isn't just a cold season, it's so many things wrapped in one,
Like how the Christmas lights that shine bright and illuminate the night,
And the stars that shine like diamonds in the cold, bleak night,
With your lips lighting up with joy at the sight of hot cocoa on your lips to keep you warm and nice,
While watching a Netflix movie, as well as doing the Christmas tree, and a jovial spirit that lies in the air,
And everyone standing there anticipating the moment to say, "Merry Christmas!" everywhere,
And you stay up till 3am waiting for good Saint Nick's reindeer,
But you then fall asleep and wake up to find presents underneath that Christmas tree,
And everyone's laughing with not an ounce of regret in the air, nothing but a gladsome atmosphere everywhere,
And everyone coming together in peace and harmony to celebrate the end of another year,
And to look back and remember all the things that have happened, good or bad, and to reflect on what your aims are for the next new year.

Priscilla-Grace Aina (14)

Happy Hannukah

In my family, there were five.
There was Mum.
There was Dad.
There was Hannah.
There was Ezra.
And there was me.
We lived for a long time
In a small, small house in Hamburg, just in
the country.

Hannah was my older sister.
She was tall, blonde, tan and beautiful.
She had big green eyes that looked like pools of
liquid emerald.
I wanted nothing more than to be just like her.

Ezra was my younger brother.
He was small, bright, and always had a
cheesy smile
Plastered across his face.
I wanted nothing more than to be free-spirited.

We had a good life.
A good enough life, I think.

Just three days after the festival of lights
That we so dearly called Hannukah,
It all went upside down.

Mum and Dad woke us up in the morning.
We children shared a room,
So it was easy for Mum's wails
And Dad's long, deep sobs to wake us up.

I let my eyes flutter open, fly across the curtains
And see that it was still dark outside.

As they cried, our dear parents let us know that we had to leave.
I did not know why, so I began to cry, as did Ezra.

Hannah comforted us and held us
Until it was time to pack our school satchels.

Mum said that we would never return.
Dad told me that we would, someday, somehow,
But I was old enough to see the remorse in

his eyes.
He was lying.

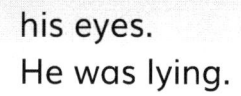

So, I stuffed in as much as I could,
So much, the zip on my bag was fit to burst.

As I stepped the last foot out of the front door,
Ushered by my parents and Hannah, I turned back.
They called me back, but it was no use.

There, on my pillow, daintily sat, my doll,
The new one, with the tanned skin, green eyes,
And long, silky blonde hair.

The next thing I knew, I was on a train.
The sun was rising in the west,
Showering my face in the bright light.

As we pulled to a stop, I read the signs,
My bleary eyes struggled to make out the letters
That were cast in iron.

Auschwitz.

I watched as we stepped out onto the platform.
I couldn't hear.
Maybe I blocked it out, or maybe there was soot in my ears.

They took Mum and Dad.
They struggled and begged to be let go,
But soon their screams sounded as though
They faded into the almost-light.

Next, they grabbed Ezra.
He seemed to lose his fiery personality in
an instant,
And I could not do anything to stop it. I cried.
I let the warm tears roll down my face, forlorn.

Then, they took Hannah.
She gave me one last pitiful smile before disappearing,
Just like the rest of my family had,
Her fair hair shone one last time in the morning light.

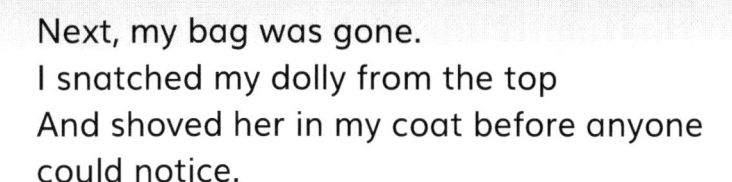

Next, my bag was gone.
I snatched my dolly from the top
And shoved her in my coat before anyone could notice.

Now there is only one person left in my happy family.
It is me.
I feel guilty every second I am alive,
That they took them and not me.

It is hardly my fault that I was blessed
With ashy-blonde hair and despairing blue eyes.
They say he likes us.
That's why he chose to spare us.

Not Mum.
Not Dad.
Not Ezra.
And certainly not Hannah.

I found it strange that the very features her life was taken for,
Were the ones that I wanted more than anything.

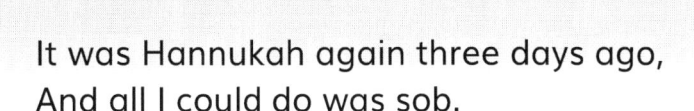

It was Hannukah again three days ago,
And all I could do was sob.

The others in my bunk shove me every time I sniff.
They warn me, "They will kill you if you make a sound."

But it doesn't matter anymore.
I would rather be dead than in Auschwitz for a moment longer.

Maybe, if I meet the same fate as my family,
We could spend Hannukah together again.
Away from here.

I held my dolly from last year tight in my arms,
Before letting out the loudest scream I had
ever heard.

The lights flicked on, and I heard marching
And undistinguished shouting.
A symphony of death and despair.

Happy Hannukah.

Liv Baker (16)

Christmas Memories

When you think of Christmas,
Do you think of snow?
I love the warmth of the fireplace glow
We fall out with friends over silly things
But under the tree, we unite and bring
Christmas is a time to celebrate and share
To show our loved ones how much we care
No matter how different we may be
The most important thing is family

When you think of Christmas,
Do you think of gifts?
I love the joy that each moment lifts
We fall out with family over old grudges
But under the tree, we forget and nudge
Christmas is a time to forgive and heal
To let go of the past and make a new deal
No matter how hard it may be
The most important thing is family

When you think of Christmas,
Do you think of food?
I love the prayer that fills the mood
We fall out with hunger over what we crave
But under the tree, we share and save
Christmas is a time to enjoy and play
To have fun with family and play games all day
No matter how hungry we may be
The most important thing is family

When you think of Christmas,
Do you think of them?
I love the memories that I keep
We fall out with fate over who we lost
But under the tree, we smile and weep
Christmas is a time to remember and grieve
To cherish the love that we still have
No matter how painful it may be
The most important thing is family

When you think of Christmas,
Do you think of white?
I love the trees shining in the night
We see furry friends, cuddling close together
As their hearts will be united forever
Christmas is a time to reflect and take note
Of the beauty in nature, the clear ice afloat
No matter how mesmerised we may be
The most important thing is family

When you think of Christmas,
Do you think of home?
A place where you won't be alone
We fall out with distance over where we are
But under one roof we shine like stars
Christmas is a time to feel and love
To be grateful for the blessings from above
No matter how far apart we may be
The most important thing is family.

Anabella Calfa (12)

While Some Animals Stay Out, Others Hibernate

S kunks are very smelly, but do they do it intentionally? Yes, they use it as a weapon to stink up their enemy and send them running scaredly.

L adybirds have lots of spots, but they're not just wearing pretty tops. Their spots are what make them unique and niche to other bugs.

E uropean hedgehogs climb trees; not like you and me. They dig their claws into the bark, in light or dark, and make their way to the tip-top. They have sharp spines, all over their body and these allow them to never feel wobbly.

E astern box turtles have red eyes but they tell lies. They can be dangerous and courageous. They can cause situations to be outrageous. Don't mess with these rangers.

P rairie dogs like walking on their hind legs and making burrows in the ground. They make a strange sound that can make you spellbound.

Phoebe Wilson (10)

The Heart Of Winter

In lands where snowflakes softly dance,
A clan resides in an icy trance,
Their haven lies 'neath frosted peaks,
Where a snow queen's plight, the heart it seeks.

Enshrined in crystal, she's confined,
A kindred soul of gentle mind,
But chains of frost hold her in sway,
Within a fortress, cold as day.

The winter wonderland, pristine and fair,
Yet shadowed by a frosty snare,
For all its beauty, a chilling hand
Grips the land 'til hearts expand.

The clan, once free in snow's embrace,
Now live in fear, a captive race,
Until one dawn, a prophecy told,
Of a heart of winter, pure as gold.

This fabled heart, a source of light,
Could shatter the darkness and end the blight,

Release the queen from frozen plight,
And bathe the land in warm respite.

Through forests deep and mountains tall,
Brave souls heed the clarion call,
Seeking whispers in the frozen air,
Guided by hope, beyond despair.

They venture forth, through snow and cold,
In search of truth, the tale foretold,
To find the heart, to break the chain,
And bring back springtime's sweet refrain.

With unity and courage true,
They reach a place where the skies are blue,
And there it lies, amidst the snow
The heart of winter, aglow with glow.

With hands extended, the heart finds rest,
A pulse of warmth, a fervent crest,
As chains dissolve and frost gives way,
The queen emerges in the day.

Her smile, a thaw, a radiant sight,
As snowflakes dance in sheer delight,

The land now bathed in newfound peace,
Winter's hold begins to cease.

The clan, now free, and the queen released,
Embrace the thaw, their joy increased,
For in the heart of winter's core,
Lies the peace they'd longed for more.

As seasons turn, and snow recedes,
The land adorned with verdant seeds,
The legacy of unity's art,
Found in the beating of a gentle heart.

Fatima Hussain (12)

In Winter's Embrace

In winter's embrace, the night's chill reigns supreme
In icy grip, where darkness finds its home,
The bitter bite of winter's breath, so keen,
Its cloak of frost and shadows ever roam,
A canvas painted in a solemn sheen.

The barren trees stretch forth their skeletal arms,
Their whispered sighs the anthem of the cold,
As moonlight weaves its spell with ghostly charms,
And stars above, in distant tales, are told.

In the silence, peaceful snowflakes gently fall,
Covers the land in stillness, hushed and deep,
Yet in this starkness, beauty stands so tall,
A solemn grandeur in the night's cruel keep.

Though bitterness pervades the wintry air,
It holds a solemn beauty, stark and rare.

Ren Owen (13)

All Throughout The Year

It's coming to the end of another fantastic year,
Drinks are held high and cheers are in the sky,
But what's happened? What's new?
What makes this year stand out to you?
Can't remember?
2023 has been a long year,
So let's rewind this year, it can surely do no wrong

January: the annually cold weather comes back yet again not only that though, but alas the world's oldest woman is put to rest,

February: earthquakes, shark attacks, bus crashes etc my memory shows all bad but not all shall be judged by that; agreements and achievements between countries are proceeding,

March: while it's dangerous in America, the weather's gone, a beaten world record for the coldest March, but surely is not as bad as the measles in Kentucky,

April: while SpaceX blows up in mid-air, fatal deaths occur everywhere

May: as finally the wetter weather grows better, lawsuits are being handed just as often, people are dying in wars,

June: as summer is finally creeping over us, trains are failing and it's not looking good for Asia,

July: while we are all chanting, "Yes, yes, yes holidays again!" horrifying gas poisonings are happening in Africa,

August: as the children are getting ready to go back to school, there is bad blood between leaders,

October: even though it's not been much fun lately, at least it comes to be Halloween, meaning time tan me off the sunscreen!

November: As the cold weather approaches yet again we shall go in the cycle once more,

December: "Hooray, hooray!" we all shout as Christmas and New Year approaches the season is arriving!

Alas, we finish the year,
Our houses covered in cotton-like snow,
A new king for Britain...
Then again we can't forget the wars,
But as Ron Weasley says best
"You can't have everything in life."

Sam Singh (11)

The Winter Memory

Snowballs whistle, sledges screech, laughter breaks the gloomy morning.
On the doorstep stands winter.
Santa's bells can be heard from the edges of the world.
Clouds pop as well as shatter, the sun comes shining through.

I look up and see powder drifting down, covering the world.
From above, a bird can view the singing trees,
They move with elegance that everybody can surely appreciate!
Skiing figures zoom by, each a little memory.

Meanwhile, a ringing silence coats itself around the houses.
Cosiness belongs to this spectacular cave.
Although at the end of the day, whole armies come marching home, wet and tired.
Later, sitting by the fire, we all enjoy our chocolate, guess from where?
Our advent calendars!

Danny Sokolov (11)

A Winter Rebirth

In winter's grasp, a girl in sorrow's plight
Her heart weighed down, lost in the cold night.
Silent tears trace the contours of despair,
Anxiety's whisper, a relentless affair.

In the hush of snowflakes, a soul entwined,
With memories of a mother, forever enshrined.
A tender voice echoes in the frosty air,
"Child, just breathe," a soothing prayer.

The icy fingers of stress begin to thaw,
As she inhales the wisdom of a love once raw.
Amidst the gloom, a flicker of hope,
A promise to cope, a resilient rope.

The winter wind whispers tales untold,
Of strength, of warmth, in the heart's stronghold.
In the stillness, she finds a sacred reprieve,
A solace that only a grieving heart can perceive.

With every breath, a step towards release,
A gentle surrender, a pathway to peace.

The snow-laden branches witness the transition.
From tears to resilience, a soul's rendition.

As frosty windows frame a world serene,
A transformation unfolds, unseen.
In the glow of holiday lights, a spirit revived,
From the depths of sorrow, she's beautifully derived.

The magic of Christmas, a balm for the soul,
Embracing the present, relinquishing control.
A dance of joy, as the snowflakes twirl,
In the arms of hope, the once-sad girl.

Her mother's words, a guiding light,
To breathe, to live, to reclaim the night.
Amidst winter's chill, a rebirth is found.
A poignant melody in the silence, resounds.

Hetvi Patel (15)

The Night's Bearer Of The Starry Halo

The flicker of light in the face of shadow,
The crackle of fire in the midst of the wintry trance.
The winter king, adorned in his crown of starry halo,
The night awaits his snow-like grace.

A faint passage of moonlight in the dark,
Giving way for all to glance at the winter king's domain.
A flurry of ice and snow ignites a spark,
In the heart, thaws a greater pain.

In the serene twilight, an ever-snowing night,
The subjects of the king, in eternal frost, recite
Poetry, and dance till dawn's first light,
In the hour of their king's majestic might.

A whirlwind of leaves, a tempest of love,
The whisper of the wind as it guides unspoken thoughts.

The unspoken thought of...
A firework of feelings, like a snowflake softly caught.

The sun and moon as they hold each other's embrace,
In turn, they illuminate the winter king's stage.
The stars are quite clear about who holds their special place,
Their performance is a spectacle on the winter king's visage.

In the dark of the mountains, the minstrel has his own way,
Weaving tapestries of the silent fall of snow.
Under the spectacle of the winter king, the people's hearts find their way,
They await the arrival of his majesty, a king whose hearts he overshadows.

In the arrival of night's rule, as winter comes and goes,
His presence brings cold smite to the weeper's tears.

For in his frosty glare resides the cold passion of which he called a ghost,
The treachery of his starry halo, a burden he alone bears.

Amelia Grala (13)

In A Winter Wonderland

In a winter wonderland, so pure and white,
Where snowflakes dance, oh what a sight!
The air is crisp, the world is aglow,
Christmas spirit fills our hearts, don't you know?

The twinkling lights, so bright and merry,
Bring warmth and joy, like a sweet cherry.
Families gather and love fills the air,
Sharing laughter, stories, and heartfelt care.

The scent of cinnamon and freshly baked treats,
Filling the house with delicious sweets.
The sound of carols, sung with delight,
Spreading cheer from morning till night.

Gifts wrapped with love, under the tree,
Bringing smiles and pure glee.
The joy of giving, the joy of receiving,
A season of love and believing.

Khloe Ndjoli (14)

Wondrous Winter

A drop of a snowflake
The drop of the rake
Children are out to play
In their flashy sleigh

Each snowflake unique
As they drop to the mountain's peak
As the first snowflake falls
Tumbling around goes the snowballs

I celebrate, especially this joyous season
And amazing is the reason
I celebrate my birthday
Even without the sun's rays

Seeing everyone so very merry
Is sweeter than a cherry
Ground clothed in holy white
Oh, what a prodigious sight

The cold is bad
But no need to be sad

Especially in the Christmas cheer
And the joy Santa brings with his deer

Everyone opens their present in delight
In the Christmas light
As January will approach
Like a travelling coach

The Christmas spirit dies down
My face forms into a frown
As my birthday slips away from clasp
I give a gasp
Of how quickly time does pass

In March it gets warmer
It's the month former
That changes from winter to spring
Quicker than my alarm ring

Winter is the time of cold
So, you need to be bold
The leaves grow once again
And vegetation will grow then

When we think of winter
The pain of it leaving is like a splinter
It goes every year
Like the most rapid reindeer

Winter will live in our hearts
The memories are like a sweet fruit tart
Never sweat
I tell you it will come again I bet.

Mary Eunice Oderanti (12)

Beloved Season

As she fell into majestic, pristine snow,
She dragged me behind her,
I rolled my eyes in exasperation,
As my new exorbitant outfit had been soaked,
I couldn't eschew the trouble,
So I raised my voice in infuriation,
A mischievous look covered her face,
Gradually uncovering a big grin,
We laughed,

Looking around I saw people amused and having fun,
This time of the year is always filled with laughter and joy,
And I too was filled with bliss and delight,
We laughed till dawn,
We enjoyed ourselves till night,
The time of year that is relished by people around the world,
Winter keeps all of the precious, cherished moments safe,
The beloved season.

Manpreet Kaur Singh (14)

The True Spirit Of Christmas!

In this little Christmas poem of mine,
I just hope to share some thoughts
And, in your mind, plant a few ideas to shine.

Christmas isn't only about the gifts we give
and get.
It's mostly about friends and family
All the loved ones we honour and won't forget.
A time of charity and kindness renewing the spirit,
To face another year to improve the soul
And strive to be a guiding angel.
To all those who need your help in any way
To lift a burden crushing them down under
its weight.

Christmas is unique to every family and following,
But one universal truth is that to our loved ones
We always strive to bring
Immense warmth and a wealth of good tidings.

Think of those who can't be with you.
With all your heart
Wish them warm flowing feelings of love
and peace
Knowing that you'll see each other again
And wrap each other in a warm embrace.

The gifts and glitter,
Glamour galore.
Are all so wonderful and exciting, bringing joy
in droves.

Christmas though is so much more.
It's of love and family and those we miss.
Embracing each other in all our love not
feeling remiss.
It's all about charity and passion
Of love and giving in our hearts.
Remember folks celebrate your true
eternal treasures
On this day of prudent depth,
And introspection on what a truly meaningful life
Entails all your deeds and greetings.

Benjamin Doeteh (17)

As We Walk

December 1st, the first snow,
She walks in, her gorgeous face is all I know,
"Shall we go on a morning stroll?"
"Of course!" I reply, my gleeful soul,
Elated to walk through Norway's North Pole,
Hand in hand with the one I love so dearly,
And off we go,
Through the whitened path,
Hidden by the snow,
As we walk, dancing snowflakes pirouette,
Left and right then straight ahead,
Before becoming puddles wet,
One falls on her head,
And I look at her again,
She looks as if her mind is elsewhere,
Her lower lip shivering and her nose is red,
I ask if she is alright,
Her reply is that she is only cold,
Yet she sounds as though she is trying so hard to be bold,
As we walk, I am reminded of my love for her,

And of the undeniable instinct to blurt to her,
How I love her so,
But what if she says no,
So, what,
If she never finds out,
I will forever bear the regretful mount,
I will do it,
"Nova, I need to tell you something."
My heart instantly beating at the speed of light,
She turns slowly as though it took all her might,
Her coiled hazelnut locks dance joyfully as do the snowflakes,
But she is not joyful,
"I do too."
She bows her head like a guilty criminal in court,
Confessing their sins,
"I'm sorry," miserable and almost pitying she adds,
As we walk up the brim of a park,
Greeted by an oak tree, it's branch like a mark,
To show hello,
But it too is lower and sympathetic,
Confused, I turned to her for answers,
Only to see nobody there.

Emma Mareva (13)

The Feeling Of Winter

I lay in my bed,
I hear whispering, whimpering
Sadness across the town spread
You're always hearing and listening.

I lay in my bed, and I dreamt,
I wished, and I wished, and I wished,
All onto a shooting star, bright
The light on my innocent hair, it kissed.

I lay in my bed, but I didn't,
And I was pondering whether I existed
I'll never know if it was real,
Or if it was all sick and twisted.

I lay in my bed, as the snow fell,
But here, I was walking in a dream.
Children were playing, love was in the air,
As the star that kissed made a beam.

I lay in my bed, as the star beamed,
Around the presents, the tree, and the sleigh,

The ice and frost chilled me to the bone,
But in that dream, I will stay.

I lay in my bed, as the carollers sang,
And the beam of light went away,
The elves and Santa Claus were all shocked,
As it was heading right for the sleigh.

I lay in my bed, all tucked up and warm,
But in that dream, I was cold.
The light shone bright, and it shone brighter
It was bright, and, oh, it was bold.

I lay in my bed, with my eyes shut tight,
As this fantasy world lost its grip,
I was falling, falling, no longer cold,
And I woke up and heard wrapping paper rip.

I was no longer in bed, with my eyes open wide,
The spirit was up, the mood was right,
It was still dark outside, but nobody cared,
Then, I saw a star, set alight.

Bella Viney (13)

The Winter Feeling

Winter might symbolise a cosy feeling.
To a different person, I'm sure
It may be the many snowflakes drifting from the inky sky.
Or when hot chocolate is suddenly appealing.
It's even supposed to be a frosty cloud forming when you sigh.
Though not for me, of course

Winter is supposed to be a warm and fuzzy feeling.
It could be cuddling closely with someone you love.
It might even mean having hands that are so numb they need concealing.
It could be marching through the snow,
Or the rivers being so icy they don't flow.

Winter could be a lot of things.
It could be being knee-deep in a blanket of snow,
Or strolling while a choir sings.
It could be rolling up a giant snowball with great force

Or baking gingerbread from handmade dough,
To someone else in the world, of course

For me, winter is something else.
Winter is the freezing wind drifting through your fingers
And making them so unbearably numb
It's the terrible weather getting to my head
Making it so hard to concentrate
On the inside, I'm practically dead
In my opinion, all winter is...
Is the horrible, icy weather freezing the tip of my ears
Winter is when the chilly smog never clears.
Winter is just cold. That's it.

And, actually, I think summer is the best feeling.

Aleena Hussain (11)

Last White Winter

The places of eternal winter have reached summertime,
Ice caps melting in the face of humanity's dreadful crime.
Think back to your last white Christmas, thick, soft snow,
Fluffy, carpeted countryside that your children will never know.
Santa's sleigh puffs out portions of pollution that the deer dine on down there,
Amongst the droughts like deserts, rising sea and dusty air.
Fast fashion thrives in winter, factories coughing up smog,
Like your cat coughs up her hairballs, 'it's a gift', no, it's just fog;
Fog that curtains the atmosphere, as the companies curtain your eyes,
"We're good for the environment," have you ever considered they're lies?
Please, think before you purchase, what consequences does it entail?

Have you ever thought of thrift shops or homemade cookies, or have you failed?
The planet needs you; don't you see? Allow the future generation some light,
Don't make them search for Santa's sleigh on grey, thick, haze-filled nights.
You can give the young people a Christmas miracle just by turning down the heat,
Buy second-hand gifts and turn off the lights, it would be such a great feat.
Be thankful for our planet as you sit around for Christmas dinner,
And you must hope it's not too late for another crisp-air, dazzling, snowy, white winter.

Chessie Young (14)

A Snowy Christmas Night

In the stillness of a snowy Christmas night,
Where moonlight dances on the glistening white,
A serene and peaceful atmosphere unfolds,
Winter's touch envelops both young and old.

Anticipation fills the air, a sense of wonder grows,
As the world prepares for the season's grand show.
Hearts flutter with excitement, spirits
shining bright,
All eagerly awaiting the arrival of Christmas night.

Streets adorned with twinkling lights, a
dazzling sight,
A symphony of colours, captivating with delight.
Homes dressed in wreaths adorning every door,
Creating a festive ambience and spreading
joy galore.

Carols resound, sung with joy and cheer,
Echoing through the air, bringing warmth so near.
Letters to Santa, filled with hopes and dreams,
As they count down the days, or so it seems.

Stockings hung with care, by the chimney's warm light,
Hoping Santa Claus will visit, bringing gifts just right.

Tables set with feasts, a culinary delight,
Roasted turkey, sweet pies, candles burning bright.
Families gather 'round, hearts grateful and in tune,
Celebrating togetherness, under the winter moon.

Yet amidst the hustle and bustle, let us not forget,
The true meaning of Christmas, a moment to reflect.
For Christmas is not just about what's been prepared,
But the joy in our hearts, and the love we share.

Ronit Gupta (12)

Winter Wonderland

In a world of frost, where snowflakes dance,
A winter wonderland, a magical trance.

Blankets of white, a shimmering sea,
Nature's artistry is a sight to decree.

Trees adorned in crystal attire,
Glistening branches, a frosty choir.

Silent whispers of a chill embrace,
Winter's magic paints each surface with grace.

The hush of snowfall, a gentle refrain,
Soft footprints are left on a crystalline terrain.

Ice-kissed lakes in a tranquil repose,
A mirror reflecting the secrets it knows.
Diamonds of frost on windows cling,
A testament to the season's zephyr swing.

The world transformed, a pristine display,
In winter's wonderland, dreams find their way.
Scarves and mittens, snug and warm,
As laughter mingles with the storm.

Fireside tales and cocoa's delight,
Cosy moments in the serene night.

A celestial dance in the northern sky,
Auroras weave a celestial lullaby.

Stars twinkle like diamonds on velvet blue,
Nature's symphony, a magical cue.
Snowflakes are unique, each a tiny piece of art,
Falling gently, a masterpiece to impart.

A frozen tapestry, a quiet grandeur,
Winter's wonderland, a timeless allure.
So, embrace the chill, let your spirit soar,
In this snowy haven, dreams galore.

A symphony of frost, a poetic swirl,
In winter's wonderland, let your heart unfurl.

Khadija Hingorani (11)

Christmas Wish

What do you look forward to on Christmas Eve?
Is it the excuse to wake up your whole family
at six in the morning?
Or the lovely Christmas dinner you're
given a plate of every year?
Do you cherish the moment
you open your presents,
Trying to guess which toy from your list
is under the wrapping?
Do you acknowledge the love and care
That has gone into every Christmas?

What if the morning of Christmas,
You'd rather hide in bed?
What if Christmas dinner,
Is it nothing but a dream to you?
What if presents under a tree,
Is nothing but a foreign concept to you?

What if you don't acknowledge the love and care,
Your parents give you,
Because you can't acknowledge what isn't there?

Your Christmas list is written on toilet paper,
With just a drawing of a happy family,
With tears blotting the outlines.
Your Christmas tree is a commercial,
Displaying countless offers on tree types,
Which your father blames you
for not being able to afford.

Your Christmas wish,
Is for Santa to visit you in your sleep
And mistake you for a lost present,
And take you far, far away from your home.

Thank your mom and dad
for such a lovely Christmas.
Children just like you wish they could.

Jaye Sayagh (14)

Christmas Reflection

Our preparation time has passed,
And a new gate has been opened for us,
And so we are ready,
To start a new beginning.

We have hope that the coming year
will be filled with joy,
And peace will fill our hearts,
Joy in our gifts,
And love from family to family.

New Year's resolutions, maybe?
A promise we make to ourselves
Both beneficial and reasonable,
A better person we could be.

What did Santa deliver this year?
A bike or a backpack,
A toy plane or a new phone,
A wish has come true.

The fun in the snow,
Laughter and joy,

Whether it is snowmen or snowballs,
We make it the most exciting.

We take part in other events,
Diwali, Hanukkah too,
With respect, we learn more about our history,
A trail of love going through our community.

Last year was a mess,
Although I have now taken a break,
And with more positivity than ever,
I happily go to the next year, the next opportunity.

Activities to take part in,
Skiing, skating or sledging,
Upbringing moments to take part in
So, come on and do not miss the fun!

Our preparation time has passed,
And a new gate has been opened for us,
And so we are ready,
To start a new beginning.

Jasmine Koc (11)

The Christmas Mouse

One winter's night,
When it was dark and cold,
A scared little mouse,
Saw a flicker of gold.

He scampered through the snow,
Leaving pawprints on the ice,
To the house with the gold glow,
That smelled of cinnamon and yule spice.

He clambered to the roof,
And down the chimney, he did tumble,
Then when he caught sight of the Christmas feast,
His little tummy started to rumble.

The gold caught his eye again,
And it filled him up with glee,
When he saw this special twinkling light,
Came from the top of the Christmas tree.

The tree was lined with lights,
And baubles of red and green,

It had tinsel wrapped around it,
A more magical thing he'd never seen.

He climbed up its stump,
And scurried over each branch,
Aiming to reach the top,
Though he didn't think he'd stand a chance.

When he finally reached the top,
A sight he did behold,
He was mesmerised and enchanted,
By the sparkling gold.

Atop of the tree,
A star did lie,
It was huge and shiny,
Brighter than any in the sky.

And on that shining star,
A wish the mouse did make,
To remain happy and playful,
And to have a belly full of cake.

So, if a mince pie goes missing,
Check the top of your tree,

For next to the star,
They may be a mouse for you to see!

Heidi Gottschall (12)

Winter

Winter, you're always cold
When are you ever going to get old
You are here from November to February
Sometimes it feels like you never go

You're here dust till dawn
Sometimes the sun likes to peek in and give us warmth
Snow comes falling down some days to give us freezing cold
Hands and feet are numb after touching snow

It's really dark and cold, I drank hot chocolate to make me feel warm
I cuddled up in a blanket to make sure I was cosy and extra warm

Sometimes the snow comes down and the sun awakes to wash it down
Ice skating is really fun in winter (not till you fall)
And many times you can't fall asleep because of the cold breeze.

Umaymah Hussain (10)

Dear Humanity

Dear Humanity,
You misunderstand me.
You love all the seasons;
Summer is warm and fun,
Spring is fresh and new,
Autumn is cosy and colourful.
Yet I am harsh and cold.
You love all the seasons; except me.
Those who celebrate Christmas tolerate me.
Until the new year.
And Christmas isn't even a part of me;
Just an optional accessory.
After that,
I'm depressing for you all.
You say I'm harsh and cold, and shield yourselves from my touch.
I'm just trying to hug and kiss your face the way summer does.
But you don't like it when I do that.
I tried to make myself pretty with white fluffy snow and glistening frost.

Then I was blamed for being slippy, making people ill.
Dangerous.
However summer is not half as feared for its dangerous heat.
Summer feels good.
Summer is so cool that its flaws melt in your eyes.
You say I'm too dark.
Sorry.
It's just that the dark makes me feel safe,
I can hide.
I'm sorry if you think I'm clingy,
I only stay so long because I can't stand to be alone.
But you've taken matters into your own hands,
Heating me,
Pushing me away.
The point I'm trying to make is, I'm not harsh and cold,
You froze me out.
Yours unfaithfully,
Winter.

Phoebe Allen (17)

Joy Of Christmas

Every Christmas, a doorbell rings;
To welcome his family and kin
Spirits are merry, spirits are high,
To welcome the vibrance within.

She opens the door and lets them in,
A grin of joy on her chin.
Before seeing a homeless man,
Looking for food from a dirty bin.

Her grin turns into a frown.
Her heart is melancholy and morose.
She forgets about the family dinner,
However, she couldn't let that door close.

She begs the man to come over,
And he obeys her command.
She tells him to come in
To go and wash his filthy hands.

As he did this,
She said, "Someone will be joining us today."

He sits down at the table.
Before eating, they begin to pray.

Mince pies adorned the table,
A large stuffed turkey in the centre.
Chocolate puddings on every plate.
As it was Christmas, in December.

They ate the food,
And drunk the finest juice.
"I'm full," was said frequently.
As they all were excused.

Clearly, they had a wonderful time,
One of the best times of their lives.
They exchanged gifts and hugs,
And a dozen high-fives!

Some people you meet have a lasting impression,
Some pass through without a mention.
The ones that stand out
Leave us no doubt
Friendships for life are without an exception.

Imose Osarhiemen (11)

Oh Christmas Tree!

It's
Christmas!
My time to shine.
The lights are twinkling.
The star, my headpiece shines,
a beacon for all to see.
People are dancing all around.
Laughing, singing, smiling and dancing.
Men and women, old and young, tall and short,
Celebrate this annual festive time
of cheer and family.
Singing peace and goodwill to all mankind.
I stand tall and proud at the heart of the festivities.
Dressed in my finest hues of
red, gold, white and cream.
My branches are a fantastical banquet for the
eyes, making me
The talk of the town. I hear them singing my
praises and giving me gifts
Repeating the phrase,
"O' Christmas tree" and smiling.

The band is playing and the carollers
are singing loud and clear.
Telling the tales of Christmas past as they
sing all the Christmas favourites.
Bringing back a feeling of childhood nostalgia as
well as a hope for the future.
Families and friends gather around the fires to
celebrate the Christmas season.
I look down at their cheerful, happy faces
glistening in the flames.
I embrace my time here in the centre.
I bask in the attention that I am given.
Soon, my time here will have finished.
But for now happy holidays one and all!

Chloe Russell (15)

Its Name Was Winter

A creature would visit these lands each year
And each year, its cold would blister.
The creature would nip and bite at the ears
And its name was Winter.

It left blizzards of frost in its wake
The air around it became much thinner
Everyone began to tremble and quake
And its name was Winter.

Animals feared its presence; they hid when they saw it
Under the weight of snow, branches would splinter.
Plants could not survive when the freeze hit
And its name was Winter.

One day, the little fox asked its mother,
"If Winter is so bad, why does it come each year for so long?"
The vixen replied in the small burrow they hid under,
"Ah, listen closely; for I will sing you Winter's song.

Indeed, the creature's cold would hurt
But it cooled the Earth, you see, despite the blister
The creature's snow would melt and hydrate
the dirt
And its name was Winter.

Indeed, the creature made us hide when we saw It
But this let us rest for the new year, despite the cold's bitter
The creature let us sleep, in our comfy burrows sit
And its name was Winter.

So that's why, little one,
The creature could indeed have been a hinder,
But it also prepared us for the new year's dawn,
And its name was Winter."

Aurelia Littlejohn (15)

A Winter Tradition

Winter is a season that we all love
A time when we can give each other a warm hug
There's one tradition that we all share
A certain kind of magic in the air!

Christmas day! That's the way!
Excitement from when we get out of bed
Dreams of the day stuck in our head
A winter tradition once a year!

Snowy walks with the dog
Times we can see the fog
Wrapped up in our scarf and mittens
We won't be seeing any kittens!

What a festive time of year
Santa Claus we cannot hear
Going to bed on Christmas Eve
A winter tradition we all believe!

Chocolate and sweets
Lovely treats
Lights and zero fights

Advent calendars
From the start of December

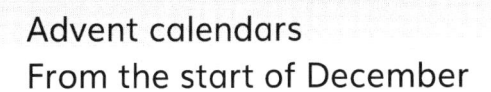

Putting up the Christmas tree
Pretty sights that we can see
Last minute shopping
Christmas themed bopping

The Christmas way! Every day!
December is the month
December is the time to be festive
A winter tradition!

Winter is a season that we all love
A time when we can give each other a warm hug
There's one tradition that we all share
A certain kind of magic in the air

Merry Christmas everyone, everywhere!

Paige Munn (9)

Winter Time

The clock ticked 12,
I looked under the Christmas tree,
My parents' mistletoe made me look away,
Pretending to barf, making my parents laugh.

Running down the stairs,
Sister's hand linked with mine,
My little brother was already demolishing his cereal.
My sister neatly unwrapped her new Beats headphones
As my dad was flashing his sideways phone in her face for a reaction.
My mum took all the rubbish in a big, black bin bag
As my little brother was destroying the wrapping paper,
"Hot Wheels," he yelled, looking at our ceiling,
"Thank you, Santa!"
I smiled as I unwrapped my rectangle-shaped gift.
A pretty, pink Barbie, I've been dreaming of since I was three.

British Sunday roast, a crisp new year for a
new start.
The snow was falling,
Thick white on the ground.
A phenomenal thing in England.
We ran out of the house,
Our scarts, boots and jackets zipped to the top,
Sand toys in hand.
Shovelling snow in the buckets,

Emptying it on my sibling's heads.
A snowman formed after some hard work,
Bright, big orange carrot standing out in the pure,
white garden.

Maria Ivescu (12)

A Christmas Countdown

Everyone's decorating with so much glee,
We gotta wrap the tinsel around the tree,
Snowflakes falling everywhere,
But no one can find the fairy lights anywhere,

Snowmen are smiling,
Children are waiting,
Letters to Santa are piling,
We're gonna go ice skating,
Everyone's excited for presents,
There's a moon in the shape of a crescent,

It's Christmas Eve and I can't believe,
Everyone wearing long sleeves
Because it's so cold;
We're putting milk and cookies on the table,
We're waiting for Santa to come,
My brother's left him a bagel,
When we come back, I bet there's gonna
be crumbs,

It's Christmas!
The best month of the year,
Time to see if we were naughty or nice all through the year,
I hope I don't get coal, one thing I fear,
Time to see the presents I got,
I got a little bot,
The snow has fallen and the day is done,
Now we've had all the fun,
It's time for the new year!

Maria Miah (11)

The Snow With No Show

It's Christmas time and Santa has arrived.
Presents under the tree staring at me.

But there's one thing missing.
Every year we expect it.

It's white.
It's soft.
It's as exciting as can be.

But this year, it's not here.

Where shall it be?
Is it under the tree?
Is it on a shopping spree?

But this year it's not here.

Is it running late, perhaps meeting
with the weather?
Oh, snow, oh, snow, where shall you be?

Maybe it's slept in this year.
Oh, Santa, oh, Christmas, oh my Christmas tree
Please tell me where it must be.
Night has fallen but the snow isn't here.
I stand, I cry, "Oh, snow, where can you be?"
I watch a shooting star zoom past me.
I wish for snow to come back this year.
Oh, I must sleep, hot chocolate puts me to sleep.

Morning has arrived.
It's white outside
It looks soft outside
The snow is here.
It's as glittery as can be.

Harley Morris (13)

Celestial Carols: A Christmas Eve Tale

Under the canvas of the Christmas Eve night,
Stars twinkle with a celestial light.
A tapestry is woven with threads of white,
Guiding the lost, in the silent night.

Stars, like beacons, in the vast expanse,
Lead the way with their radiant dance.
To the wise men, they gave a glance,
A celestial guide in their advance.

In the heart of winter's cold embrace,
Stars illuminate the infinite space.
A symbol of hope for the human race,
A promise of dawn, a new day's grace.

The journey of the wise men, so divine,
Guided by the star's holy sign.
To Bethlehem, under the star's design,
A testament of faith, forever enshrined.

Stars, they whisper to the silent night,
Of a Saviour born under their light.
A story of love, of God's might,
Echoed in the stars, this Christmas night.

So, look up to the starlit sky,
See the celestial bodies passing by.
In each star, a story lies,
Of hope, of love, under the Christmas guise.

Eisha Tajammal (18)

Christmas And Friends

C hristmas is usually with family, but I disagree.
H ere at home, all snug and warm,
R epetitive laughter runs through the house.
I mportant notice: the band is back together!
S tay for the party, will you?
T hough family is important, we have to appreciate what friends do.
M any people say family is the most important thing, but that isn't always the case
A nd friends always get left behind at Christmas, like old smartphones getting thrown in a drawer.
S ee what I mean and look at the importance of friendship, what it means to you

F amily and friends should be included in Christmas, whatever happens in time
R aining outside on Christmas Day? Friends will be there to help
I nteresting chats with them all day long
E verybody should be included at Christmas, family or friends

N othing stands in the way of friendship, it is an unbreakable bond
D o you think the same as me?

Alice Talbot (10)

A Runaway

It is night already in my room
The darkness from outside shines.
I am alone, the fear in me rises.
But outside is a whole new world.
A place to play and enjoy
A winter wonderland is the word.

I close my eyes and enter a bright light.
The fear in me vanishes and now I have sight.

The snow and the frost I touch with my bare hands.
Surprisingly, it is not cold.

My excitement jiggles up and about
Because I am not affected by the snow.
What an amazing dazzling show.

I run towards the woods with no care in the world.
I was a one-man herd.

I skip and I hop and there I stop.
To my horror, a beast lies down.
Sleeping as if it had never had rest.

Was I to flee? Well, the answer must be yes.
So, I walk quietly and try my best.

But the fear in me will not shut.
The beast moves slightly.
And there was a churn in my gut.

Was I to be eaten alive?
The beast's eyes open...

Danielle Erikume (10)

The Flame Of Hope

The hope that glows like a flame in a fire,
Lighting up the darkness of our hearts,
A curling flame that traces out the lines of our lives.

Crafted in the careful hands of a blacksmith,
The most delicate metal ever created,
Silver, gold, a pinky hue,
Pretty, perfect, scary, strong.
Able to change fate,
To sculpt our futures,
Our lives are painted in the palm of its hand,
A mix of colours and swirls.
As we age and grow,
It changes our journeys and lives,
Making me the person I am meant to be,
And you, the person you are meant to be.

It comes when we most need it,
Like an angel or a deity,
On the cold night of Christmas Eve, it swoops in,
And lays out a flavoursome feast for our souls.

Its fire melts the icicles,
The ones in the snow-covered gardens,
And the ones inside of us,
The purest Christmas gift.
And once the Christmas period has passed,
And we enter another year,
It's what gives us the strength to not give up,
And to pass on hope.
To pass on the flame.

Isabelle Poulton (12)

My Favourite Time Of Year

Hear the crunching of leaves,
Feel the soft snow up to your knees.
See the foxes,
Wrap all the presents in little boxes.
Feel the joy,
Watch the boy open his new toy.
Smell the mulled wine
Or the hot chocolate that smells divine.

Watch the stars above,
With those who you love,
While being wrapped up in a blanket,
Dreaming of a Christmas banquet.

This is the time for celebrations and cheer,
And also for colds and waiting for Santa to appear.
For sitting on the couch to watch a movie,
And for Dad telling you that his dance moves are groovy.

Winter is my favourite time of year,
Even if the cold hurts my ear.
Sitting by the fireplace and reading a book,
Waiting for the turkey to cook.

Hear the crunching of leaves,
Feel the soft snow up to your knees.
See the foxes,
Wrap all the presents in little boxes.

Feel the joy,
Watch the boy open his new toy.
Smell the mulled wine
Or the hot chocolate that smells divine.

Amie Varley (14)

Contrast Of Light And Dark

Trees decked with silver and gold
The wind swirls around me
Left out in the cold
It is not too hard to see
The contrast of light and dark
All it will take is one spark

Candy canes litter the path
Gifts clutter the rooms
All suffer the wrath
He lived to read his own tomb
The contrast of light and dark
All it will take is one spark

"Birth of the Lord!" they'll cry
Call to His people
Angels flock so high
For one of the steeples
The contrast of light and dark
All it will take is one spark

Snow will fall to the ground
Voices in the street
Silent yet so loud
Touch the pavement, ice to sleet
The contrast of light and dark
All it will take is one spark

Immanuel to be born
Perfection on Earth
Like Isaiah was sworn
Given by God, The Son's birth
The contrast of light and dark
He is the one spark

But this world is too cruel
And so full of sin
We could not see the jewel
For he dwelt within
The contrast of light and dark
Why could we not hark?

Mackenzie Shurmer (14)

Winter's Echoes

In the city where lights shine so bright,
A story unfolds on a cold, dark night.
Beds made of concrete, dreams feeling old,
People outside, winter's freezing hold.

Christmas songs play, but not for all,
Some folks hurting and feeling small.
Whispers in alleys, a heart's quiet plea,
In the city's heart, where no one sees.

Faces show stories of hard, tough days,
City beats loud, in so many ways.
Snow falls soft on cardboard floors,
Telling tales of struggles and closed doors.

City lights flash, stores full of cheer,
Some folks missing, not feeling near.
City's heartbeat, a quiet sound,
Homeless souls on the cold ground.

Christmas cheer, like a distant hum,
Asphalt echoes, where shadows drum.

Let's break the silence, hear their call,
In these streets, where hearts enthral.

Shelter not just in walls so tall,
But in kindness shared, love for all.
In these streets where stories blend,
Feel the warmth, let hearts transcend.

Safia Ali (17)

Twinkling Dreams On Christmas Eve

Snowflakes falling soft and light,
Christmas Eve is a magical night.
The world outside all dressed in white,
I'm waiting for Santa, oh so tight!

Twinkling lights in every street,
Stockings hanging, oh, what a treat!
Cookies left for Santa's sweet,
And dreams of presents, oh, so neat!

In my jammies, cosy and snug,
I'll dream of reindeer giving a shrug.
Tomorrow's the day, oh, the Christmas hug,
Presents waiting under the tree rug!

Through the window, the moon's so bright,
Casting shadows in the silent night.
I close my eyes, hold on to the sight,
Can't wait for the morning, oh, it's so right!

Gifts with ribbons, shiny and curled,
In the morning, they'll be unfurled.
Christmas joy in a snowflake world,
Excitement and giggles, let them twirl!

So here I am, tucked in so tight,
Dreaming of Christmas, oh, what a sight!
Snowy night, stars shining bright,
Tomorrow's the day, can't sleep tonight!

Het Patel (8)

Grandad, Are You There?

Waiting for that ring,
At the end of the line,
To hear your voice,
Each and every time,
Now that line is unused,
And I am left confused,
Hello, are you still there,
Grandad, I can't hear you,
Why did you leave me?
The time I thought we had,
Clearly deceived me,
The need to feel your touch,
Am I asking for too much?
As all I feel is the grief,
That cages me,
The darkness evermore,
Which I used to adore,
Now I look for you in it,
Trying to saviour our last memory,
When your eyes were destined but free,
Now Christmas rolls around again,

Unable to wish with any sincerity,
A reminder,
The joy of Christmas I surrender,
As you are all I remember,
The empty atmosphere,
Where your shadow stays,
Wishing for a sign that you're still here,
With me,
Never letting your soul disappear,
As I know you will always be near.

Isabelle Trilloe (15)

The Spirit Of Christmas

Three little children playing in the snow,
Their hands are red and their faces aglow,
With the spirit of Christmas, and letting everyone know,
That Santa's coming, 16 hours to go!

Church bells ring, shaking the ground,
Sprinkling the season with the beautiful sound,
Of choirs singing, the faint smell of frankincense all around,
Remembering the life of Jesus Christ, at birth, king he was crowned.

Ring out the old, ring in the new,
For when Christmas is over, a new year is due,
Lights on houses, in the darkness of night, shine through,
Guiding the lost spirits into the new year, pristine promises pursued.

Christmas is for giving, for showing that we care,
For our happiness and love, the time that we share,

For bathing in the magic, sailing through the air,
For reminding ourselves to look for The Spirit of
Christmas, for it will always be there.

Athena Campbell (14)

The Man Behind The Mask

A smile so deceitful,
An existence so dreadful.
A complexion so dull,
A monstrosity untold.
Eyes so consuming,
Spirits so dooming,
The man behind the mask, the one who seems strong,
A man who seems to be all in the wrong.
The story behind it only he knows,
As his story only starts to unfold...
He seems like a creature yet not so bold,
An ego so high,
Misunderstood.
On one Christmas day, things start to change
Unspeakable things that were so very strange.
As time goes by he starts to unravel,
As the spirits from the past come to time travel.

They teach him a lesson that no one could,
As shame and self-pity there it stood.
An old friend came to visit who was presumed to be dead,
As the man behind the mask was speechless,
he said.
A man so persistent in his ways not words
But only the supernatural could change,
The man was then left with his emotions uncaged.
The man with those spirits so cold,
The name was Scrooge and now his story unfolds...

Rida Jaffery (14)

Crisp Canvas Of Winter: Nature's Masterpiece

The world is asleep, a blanket of ice white,
Pale, dull light etched across bare trees.
Not any vivid greens, no flowery displays,
Just the stark, sleeping hosts of nature.
Where birdsong swirled, now silence robs its riches.
A hush falls, a frosty breath. A still pond, a frozen stream,
A planet buried and its mysteries sealed away.
However, beauty shines with a crystal sheen
As sunlight turns the snow into a brilliant diamond.

Icicles that are like prisms catch the heavens
And frost-laced boughs that rise like sculptures.
Life sleeps deep, patient, and full of longing beneath the snow,
Where a secret fire resides.
The pledge preserved in ice,
As spring retreats, verdant shoots.
So let us stroll into winter's grasp,

Our hearts are open to the revelations still to be revealed.
For the quiet of winter,
A lullaby that clings to unfading hope.

Nishtha Ghelani (13)

The Stars' Guide

Beneath the cloak of Christmas Eve's embrace,
A tapestry of stars adorns the cosmic space.
They twinkle in a celestial ballet,
Guiding wayfarers on their journey's array.

Silver sparkles against the midnight hue,
A celestial choir, a radiant view.
In each gleaming orb, a tale unfolds,
Of hope reborn, as timeless stories are told.

The North Star, a beacon in the velvet sky,
Whispers of promise, a lullaby.
It guides the wanderers, both near and far,
A compass of dreams, a cosmic memoir.

Amidst the constellations, stories align,
Echoes of ancient tales, shimmering signs.
As travellers look to the heavens above,
Stars weave tales of courage, of enduring love.

A celestial dance, a symphony of light,
On Christmas Eve, a magical night.

The cosmos whispers secrets untold,
Of beginnings anew, of futures to unfold.

Gracie Allen (14)

Winter's Last Kiss

My love will be gone by this winter
Mental pain to think and the bleak moving process we'll have to go through
All memories shared are memories never forgotten
Laughs and cries the two of us have shared
So many moments we have enjoyed in bed
In spring we were fine
In summer it took a turn
In autumn it was declining
Now winter, the ride is nearly over
Hovering over him as I take his hand in mine
Squeeze it hard for the very last time
I try not to cry but he tells me not to
He wants me to be happy and said I shouldn't be living like this
He loves me, he loves me, breathes those final words
And then, no sound could be heard
Days later, I'm at his funeral
I cry, I cry, I weep my eyes

He's up there looking down on me I want
to believe
Snowflakes hit my skin ever so softly
This, I know, is winter's last kiss.

Livie Johnston (14)

The Excitement Of Winter Time

Dandelions swayed and danced away,
Spreading their seeds for the rest of the day.
Thick jumpers came on,
And the shorts were gone.
Five o'clock and it was already dark,
I had no more time left to play in the park.
Around me, candles were lit,
As I found somewhere to sit.
Fireworks exploded,
As soon as they were reloaded.
Chocolate ripped open twenty-four days in a row,
But soon all of them would go.
Carols sung,
Mistletoe hung.
Winter Wonderland coming,
My heart started pouncing.
I was lured,
As screams were heard.
Off came my mittens,

As churros were eaten.
Christmas trees decorated,
Wish lists were created.
Turkey first,
Then crackers burst.
New Year's Resolutions were made,
Schools paid.
Uniforms worn,
Children's hearts are torn
Snow slushing,
Days increasing.
Coats in cupboards,
Spring birds.
Trees with leaves,
Shorts back on knees.
Goodbye, old year,
Hello, new year.

Siddhant Gupta (13)

Whims Of Winter

It came from nowhere
Hinted at its arrival
Nipping our fingers and cheeks a rosy pink
Frosted over our streets and windows
As to say
I'm on my way

A crisp dawn
A warm embrace
Blankets of white swathed the town
Avian curiosity traced the ground
Marvelling at this thing we call snow

Rosy cheeks
Roads adorned in white
Fingers became gloved
And snowballs commenced the fight
Glee is heard at each hurdle
Children's footprints, a crisp chorus,
seeking surprise

Atmosphere becomes frost
And the water ice kissed
Chilled hearts thawed
Innocent weather fosters innocence
And love to flow through once again

'Til the sun's swift arrival at dawn
Bidding the snow's farewell in a hurry
Vanishing like a transient guest
Reserving surprise visits for another day.

Hanna Elkaram (18)

Christmas

Christmas is when you,
Celebrate the birth
Of Christ, the son of God.

Happiness and joy,
Holidays and toys,
Having fun is the most important thing of all.

Ribbon-topped presents
Are right under the tree,
Resting beside the fireplace.

On this holiday,
On this day,
In a circle, we sing away.

Stockings are full of surprises,
Santa must've visited from the North Pole,
Soaring in his magical sleigh.

Together we sit
As treats are given around,
The tinsel-decorated table.

Morning rises,
Merry Christmas to all,
Mistletoe hangs on the wall.

Waiting is over,
For my advent calendar is done,
Another year left until the next Christmas.

Scintillating baubles shine around the house,
Stars fill the sky,
Six more days until the new year begins.

Abira Loganathan (11)

The Gift Of Christmas

Christmas, Christmas, a magical glow,
A tale of this time I show below.
With holiday gifts a glimpse of delight
A poem of Christmas shining so bright.

Snowflakes descend, a tiny sachet,
Whispering secrets, as they melt away.
Chimneys breathe out smoke in the air,
As people prepare for reindeer there.

A tree grows again at the start of spring,
Maybe we should all rise and sing.
Candles dim, casting a warm, golden fume,
Illuminating hearts, as Santa breaks through.

Candles relight, voices in song,
Bouncing tunes, both tender and strong.
Bells ring in cities, announcing the cheer,
Drawing our loved ones near.

Children's laughter, like waves in the sea,
Anticipation dances, their hearts at ease.

Stockings hang bulging with surprises,
Eyes wide with excitement, their temptation arises.

Bobby Dearing (11)

Winter's Beauty Unveiled

In frosty shroud, where whispers roam,
A winter tale finds its cherished home.
Upon the stage of snow-kissed scenes,
A symphony in white, pure and serene.

The dance of flakes, a delicate waltz,
From heavens high, where wonder exalts.
Each snowflake, a gem in twilight's gleam,
Painting a canvas in a silent dream.

The trees stand tall, in icy attire,
Their branches adorned, a crystal choir.
A world enchanted, in a frosty embrace,
A whispered sonnet, in nature's grace.

Yet 'neath the chill, a warmth resides,
In hearts entwined, by firesides.
A cosy haven, where kinship's found,
With laughter's echo, joy profound.

The wintry hush, a tranquil balm,
As nature weaves its silent psalm.

An award to winter's mystic trance,
In its frozen beauty, a timeless dance.

So let us toast this snowy delight,
In its elegance, a breathtaking sight.

Pia Patel (13)

The Wonder Of Winter

Cold and dark outside
Huddling close inside
Blankets spread and a fire lit
This will be the perfect winter night

A cup of tea
Or some hot chocolate
A gift to open
It's sure to be a thrill

Decorations hung
Wrapping paper strewn
The perfect time to be
Together with those you hold dear

Let the merriment begin
Laughter, smiles and fun
A time now to be lived in turn.

Twinkling lights
On the front porch
Sleigh pulled by a reindeer

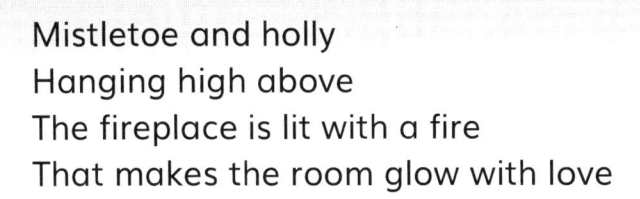

Mistletoe and holly
Hanging high above
The fireplace is lit with a fire
That makes the room glow with love

The elves are busy
Preparing gifts for
Christmas Eve
Wrapping presents
While their tiny fingers are
Nimble and spry

The air is still
The snow is thick
And outside I hear
The sound of sleigh bells that chime

So please come in
And join the fun
This holiday is meant for everyone.

Nadia Sysak (13)

Three Trees In The Moonlight

Three trees shivered
In the cold moonshine
A date palm, an olive
And a dark green pine

They whispered together
Saw a light in the sky
Paused, secrets forgotten
Heard a new baby's cry

They stood in the yard
Near the child's manger bed
"What can we give him?"
The gentle pine said.

The olive gave oil
To soothe his small feet
The palm promised dates
All sticky and sweet

"But what about me?"
The poor pine tree cried
"I can't think of a thing
I've tried and I've tried"

Hearing her cries
All the stars tumbled down
To light up her branches
Like a bright golden crown

Then the pine tree stood tall
So the baby could see
On that first Christmas Day
His first Christmas Day.

Daniel Irfan (9)

A Christmas Day

On the first day of Christmas, my mum woke me up
And said, "Do you know the special event today?"
She helped me up and gave me a hot chocolate milk cup

It was Christmas day and I asked my mum if I could play
"No," she replied, "because we have to unwrap the presents.
I said, "Can't I unwrap the presents later, Mum?"
My mum said I made Christmas breakfast and there was a lavender scent
She also said, "Food is ready, we are going to have a nice meal, come!"

Santa! Santa jumped into the chimney and ate the mince pie
He took the carrot and fed it to his one and only Rudolph!
Santa looked tired
Then he said, "Well, ho, ho, ho! I've got to go, bye-bye!"

Santa made a sprint and sprinted off...
Back to the North Pole!

Akshayan Vivekanantharajah (7)

The Catastrophe Before Christmas

It was the night before Christmas when all were abed
Expecting presents the very next day.
At the North Pole on that very same night,
Santa was getting ready for a flight.
With presents and presents in his sack on his sleigh,
He had to give all of them before it was day.
He flew his reindeer across the night sky,
Forgetting one present, oh dear, oh my.
He flew around the world realising not the present he left.
He gave 1,000 presents when he was supposed to give 1,001
Santa said, "Oh no!" after realising what he had done.
He searched and searched for the present he left
He searched the North Pole and found where it was at dawn.

He rushed and rushed across the dawn sky
He gave the last present in the nick of time, thank goodness.
It was finally Christmas.

Thomas Cassidy (8)

Winter Memories

Don't you remember the winter memories?
Of the times we used to play,
Throwing snowballs at each other,
Almost every day.

Don't you remember the winter memories?
Of the times we used to shake,
Realising we should have worn our coats,
What a silly mistake.

Don't you remember the winter memories?
Of the times we used to make,
Our very own snowman, Ellie was his name,
And how long it would take.

Don't you remember the winter memories?
Of the times we used to slide,
Across the ice, laughing about,
Until I fell and cried.

Don't you remember the winter memories?
Of how we were so keen,

To play together in the cold,
And enjoy the snowy scene.

Don't you remember the winter promise?
The one that we both agreed to,
That no matter what we would play,
In the winter, just me and you

Adetomi Adeyemi (11)

Christmas Stars Illuminate Dreams

Beneath the velvet Christmas Eve sky,
Stars emerge, a celestial lullaby.
Guiding wise men with shimmering light,
Hopeful beacons in the silent night.

A cosmic dance in the vast expanse,
Each star is a promise, a chance.
Wisdom written in constellations bright,
A celestial map, a guiding light.

In the east, where the Magi tread,
Stars whispered secrets overhead.
A cosmic tale, ages unfold,
A journey etched in stars, stories untold.

Nebulas weave dreams of ancient lore,
As galaxies hum carols to adore.
The heavens declare a birth anew,
A cosmic gift, a promise true.

Gaze upon the sky, each twinkle, a guide,
An interstellar journey where dreams reside.
In the tapestry of the celestial sea,
Christmas whispers, "Believe and be free."

Maggie-May Prior (15)

A Wonderful Winter Walk

I walk outside and see the snow,
As I hear the frosty winds blow,
I feel chilly and my fingers are numb,
As I see more children start to play and come,
There are small little snowflakes way up high,
As I see a robin and I start to sigh,

The trees are wearing glamorous snow coats,
There in the corner, sits a mountain goat,
Everyone is happy here,
So why do I still feel so queer?

I hear lots of children starting to laugh,
I go to join them on the icy path,
We walk down, towards a frozen lake,
Oh, what a winter we can make!

On the ground, there falls more ice,
It was starting to feel really nice,
Slosh, *crush*, *splash* my feet go,
The point of winter had started to show,

Inside, I am feeling much less queer,
I am in a mood of cheer!

Ivaanya Marwah (12)

Bargain With Evil

Made a bargain with the devil
He said he wouldn't meddle
Kept my foot on the pedal
But I knew he wouldn't settle

Made a deal with hell
Next thing was a wedding bell
Made one wish upon a well
From which a dream I fell

Made a promise to my love
As sweet as heaven's dove
Swore that I would never shove
Told her to always aim above

An angel flew down to me
Helped me, made me see
That one like me could not be free
I laughed and smiled with glee

I told him that as I am always here
The humans shall never fear

Of monsters and scared bear
To live and always share

We nodded and turned to leave
Before asking if I really believe
I told him, my eyes would never deceive
On that fatal Christmas Eve.

Aden Fincken (15)

Robin

Didn't anyone tell you
Where the robin's red breast is from?
The bleak mid-winter was warmed
With this tale, we've told for so long
The cross was covered in red,
The blood that Jesus had spilt
And the bird perched upon his head
Watching, waiting, and still

If you are patient for your time,
To seize this life we live
And light the Yule log fire
Watch it, as the red-breasted robin did

He stood for a while, bound in holly and 'toe
Beyond understanding is the truth,
But the bird eventually had to go

And when he flew, he flew,
And when he did he went high,
To show the winter sun
The one you see in the sky

His breast was stained with blood
Or wine, or rose petals, and thereof,
The little robin's red breast was stung,
With the colour of hatred, injury,
But most of all, the colour of love.

Grey Mazillius (14)

Winter

The cold on your face is bitter
The sky is made out of glitter
The dark night is drawing in
The ice on the ground is slippy and thin

The snow glows white
Bringing the cold tonight
Winter is here
The children come out
They start to run about

Coats have been worn
Presents have been torn
Heating is turning
Fire is burning

Winter is coming
Christmas is loving
This is a reason
Winter is a season

Winter seasons have arrived
Leaves on the trees have now died

Snow and rain are many blasts
Sunny days are in the past

Christmas trees have filled the room
Christmas presents are in the loom
Mild times now the few
Cards now are sent too

Christmas toes are tapping
Family members are rapping
Blustery winds are blowing
The sun is lowering.
I can't wait for the winter season.

Gurvir Sandhu (12)

A UK Christmas

All the presents are hidden away
We're banned from even looking
Mum is baking something strange
Please save us from her cooking

Everywhere you look or turn
Snow's falling all around you
Make sure to check where you next step
It's icy and slippery too

The festive feeling's everywhere
It's red and green and gold
All the girls and boys are waiting
Stood complaining. "It's too cold!"

Mariah Carey is on repeat
While we decorate the tree
The shops are nearly closing soon
It's time for a shopping spree.

Now it's Christmas Day
And the wrapping paper's everywhere

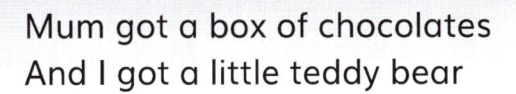

Mum got a box of chocolates
And I got a little teddy bear

Soon it will be New Year
We've made it after all
Now all I have to say is
Merry Christmas to you all.

Piper Jayne Lewis (13)

Winter Time Again

Cold, frosty, wrapped up warm
It's winter time again.
When the leaves are gone
I know it is winter time again
When plants have died and are all dried up
It's winter time again.
I really like it when it is winter time again.
Freezing snow in the air
Inside houses are warm and cosy.
Snow! Snow! Snow!
It's definitely winter time again.
The snowmen have melted
Just the carrot is left.
It's not winter time again.
I look out my window
And I see the freezing snow.
Now I know it really is winter time again.
I love it when it really is winter time again.
Do you love it too?
But there is a creature that has fifteen eyes,
Four noses and 6,000 teeth.

Don't worry because it only comes
On New Year's Eve.

Layla Saunders (9)

A Candle Flicker

Winter's crawling ever so closer,
As thee' frigid mornings and endless nights appear,
The icy and white roads we drive on,
All gone in just a candle flicker.

Winter's striding ever so closer,
As cups of hot cocoa sitting by a warm fire appear,
The snow angels and snowmen we make,
All gone in just a candle flicker.

Winter's marching so ever closer,
As the leaves turn frail
and old hanging on the trees,
And the hibernating animals lay
down their weary heads,
All gone in just a candle flicker.

Winters racing so ever closer,
As the happiness of Santa Claus
bringing the presents appears,

As your jolly neighbours dance
around this time of year,
As everything's gone in just a candle flicker.

Alanis Harrison (11)

The Figure Skater

Gracefully gliding across the endless stretch
of white,
Her heart beats faster in the spotlight.
Millions of eyes stare down at the elegant skater,
She's a master of her craft and an
inventive creator.

Smiling radiantly, she flips and loops,
As the dazzled, bewildered crowd cheers
and whoops.
She jumps highly and her landings are clean,
A champion skater she is, a true ice queen.

She skates with poise, her movements art,
A true princess, she steals their heart.
Her spirals are long, her edges as sharp as a blade,
The rays of light reflect in her eyes, the colour
of jade.

She fearlessly moves into the Biellman spin,
By now, the entire crowd wants her to win.

Her brunette hair curls, falling out of her bun,
One last twizzle turn and the dancer is done.

Laiba Sohail (14)

White Christmas

Snow is falling,
You can smell the mince pies,
The turkey is roasting,
The Christmas tree is adorned with baubles and tinsel,
The fire is going, you're opening presents then,
"Mummy, look, it is a white Christmas!"

Snow angels,
Snowmen,
Snowball fight,
Music playing,
Hands are cold,
You're covered in snow, but you don't care,

The turkey is on the table,
With sprouts,
Stuffing,
Gravy,
Bang goes the crackers,
Again *bang*,
The hats are now on,

And you read out the joke,
Now pudding,
Glorious Christmas pudding,
With warm hot chocolate
(With marshmallows, of course),
And toasty warm mince pies,
What could ever beat this?

Present time,
Gifts are unwrapped,
Even more joy on their faces,
This is the best Christmas ever.

Sarah Ward (11)

To Be A Lover At Christmas

To be a lover at Christmas,
To dance together in the snow,
To hold each other when the cold gets viscous,
To let our love forever grow.

To go to Christmas markets,
To sing Christmas songs together,
To kiss under the mistletoe,
To write cheesy letters to each other.

To be a lover at Christmas,
To go ice skating as a couple,
To never let our home be colourless,
To embrace festivities without a grumble.

To visit family on Christmas Eve,
To admire the falling snow with one another,
To drink hot chocolates, and likely swap as you won't like your own,

To exchange loving glances as the magical 'Winter Wonderland' season comes to an end.

Oh, to be a lover at Christmas.

Summer Petch (14)

Christmas Time

'Tis the best day of the year,
When happiness shines so clear.
'Tis the season to be jolly,
When the atmosphere isn't melancholy.

Children opening their present,
And fighting when parents are absent.
The best gift of all,
Is, of course, receiving alcohol!

Christmas dinner brings families together,
It also ruffles a few feathers!
Pulling crackers, sharing jokes
Followed by a screening of Hollyoaks.

Watching Christmas films to end a magical day,
Remembering Jesus Christ on his birthday.
Feeling stuffed at the end of the day,
Going to start a healthy diet someday.

'Tis the best time of the year,
When true happiness is crystal clear.

'Tis the season to be jolly,
With the blossoming of Christmas holly.

Cali Hughes (18)

Winter Wonderland

Wintertime is here,
Time to spread the joy and cheer.
We are all having fun,
With everyone!

In this season, there's a celebration,
Which we celebrate throughout the nation.
It is called Christmas,
At this time of year, we ask for forgiveness.

A naughty elf will arrive,
But there could be five.
He will see how nice you are,
To tell Santa!

We all really love to ice skate,
It feels great.
Some people like sledging,
But make sure you know where you're heading!

Santa Claus comes down the chimney,
No one should be watching Disney.

Gives presents to those who are nice,
But naughty people get mice...

Ayat Waseem Khan (8)

Winter's Wonders

Snow.
It's the first thing I see
The ground turns white
And it pleases me

I gaze at the icicles
I'm in dismay
But everything aside the winter
Never bothered me anyway

I turn around,
And beam at my mum
This is a wonder
I haven't seen in so long.

I adore snow, icicles and seeing my breath
It helps me feel alive
It makes me think of
How I'm able to survive

I live with the cold,
I walk through white.

I'm pleased tenfold
I feel quite alright.

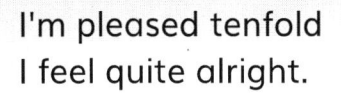

Snow.
It's something I love.
As the winter comes,
You'll see me run tonight.

Taifa Rawza (12)

Savage Sky

December 1960
It is damp.
The kind of dampness that hangs in the air but
it is humidity.
It is the kind of dampness that comes before
the rains,
miniature raindrops dot on our cheeks and noses.
The start of a great storm.
There is a cloud above.
The kind of cloud that can make the world go
black and white.
Not even the most colourful leaves
or the most brightly lit Christmas tree could look
colourful in this weather.
It is not necessarily a black cloud.
More like a grey sheet.
A cloud of a thousand shades.
The wind punches our faces and rattles in our ears.
Throwing us back to where we used to belong.
This was going to be a long winter.

Scarlet Carr (11)

The Hearth

Every winter the same argument arises.
As the fire in the hearth dwindles,
You turn to me with
Sparks in your eyes and a glow
In your countenance.
"The sun shall grace my return"
You would claim with glee.
And whilst I would try to diminish it
The idea and resolve have already burst
Its vessels
And you are walking out the door
Your jacket half-zipped, gloves long forgotten.
A grin accompanies you as you traipse
The frozen lake, nonchalant
To the wintertide whispers whilst
The windows fog up.
Knocking at the door with scraped hands,
Your smile is illuminated by the night sky,
And I fuss about the mess you brought.
Yet, as the condensation drips,
My transient complaints fall to nought.

Gabriella Rundle-Shahzad (16)

A Christmas Wish

When the night falls,
To the reindeer, he calls,
Then he comes on his sleigh,
Shouting, "Chocks away!"
The children believe with all their hearts,
That Santa is not just a work of art,
"He is real!" they all cry,
And to meet him they try,
If they are on the naughty list,
"Oh, give me a gift!", they all insist,
All the children try to be good,
As much as they possibly could,
But sometimes they are just misunderstood,
Though they attempt to do what they should,
And they are therefore good kids,
Even if they don't clean their beds,
Some kids, though not many,
In terms of gifts, they do not have any,
So remember to be nice,
And to do things without being asked twice.

Shrinjal Mishra (9)

Just Another Christmas Night

A carpet of snow fully white,
Children dreaming of Santa's flight,
Delivering presents left and right.
Sending joy all through the night.
A golden sleigh shining bright,
A wonderful fountain of pure light.

Amazing wonders he brings in his sack,
There's never anything he forgets to pack.
Filling your stocking with either a toy or snack,
Your Christmas will never ever be black,
He leaves the presents and always looks back,
Making sure they're in a stack.

He leaves presents for you to unwrap,
Your Christmas tree doesn't have a gap.
Just as his ride's energy begins to sap,
He gives one final glance at his map.
At last, he finishes his yearly lap
Now Santa really needs a nap.

Oliver Champney (11)

A Haunted Christmas

Christmas feels like Halloween,
I'm haunted.
As people pray to the angels in heaven,
I am followed by the demons.
The demons that give me anxiety, fear and stress.
As children play in the snow, the white precipitation falls
to pierce and stick inside me.
Usually, when children's hands are hurting from the cold snow I think,
Does it burn? Knowing I used all the pain
Does it hurt? Knowing it's fuel to my flame
People tell me I should laugh and smile more at Christmas
But the flames have burnt out all of it.
But I wish others a merry Christmas,
That they don't experience the darkness that some do.
Remember the angels you have.
Avoid the demons others have.

Victoria Cicha (16)

It Truly Feels Like Winter

It truly feels like winter
People can feel it in their feet
The sky pouring down sleet
The icy lakes
All covered up with snowflakes
It truly feels like winter
The streets are covered in snow
Having a hot chocolate with a single marshmallow,
Ice covering the street
Houses trying to trap the heat
It truly feels like winter
People taking part in a Christmas choir
Sitting at home and getting warm by the fire
It truly feels like winter
This year has been a blast
But at the start of a new year, we look at the past
We remember the fun times
Regret our most recent crimes
It truly feels like winter
This year has been a blast.

Amelia Barnes (13)

Goodnight Winter

There's a chill lingering in the air
People want to venture to their lair
We want something hot
Maybe it's cooking in the pot

The leaves aren't there
The trees are bare
But the nights are growing longer
We have less time to ponder

We snuggle up in our beds
Yet, our noses and toes still feel dead
We turn on our heaters
They should look a little neater

We ignore the mould
We just don't want to be cold
We get a hot drink
Careful not to spill it in the sink

Yet when summer comes
We want to feel numb

We ask, "Where are you, winter?
Oh, where are you winter?"

Yasmin Abdullah (11)

Winter Months

Skeletons and pumpkins are put away,
Our thoughts now turn to the festive holiday.
As the days get shorter and the nights draw in,
Temperatures plunge and the frost begins.

Leaves on the ground, trees stand bare,
All alone in the cold frosty air.
Preparations begin for that very special day,
The wrapping of presents is well underway.

Trees are up, presents are wrapped,
All we need now is Santa and his hat.
Time has flown by,
I can't believe we're here.
What's that I hear?
A Christmas cheer!

The festive time has been and gone,
We loved you dear,
But now it's time time to welcome the new year!

Holly Pitts (12)

Cosy Winter Nights

In winter's embrace, the world turns to ice,
A snowy wonderland, oh, so nice.
The air is crisp, the sky so clear,
As snowflakes fall and we spread cheer.

The trees stand tall, their branches bare,
A quiet beauty, beyond compare.
Footprints in the snow, a trail to follow,
Through winter's playground, we happily wallow.

Cosy fires crackle, warming our hearts,
As we gather 'round, a moment to impart.
Hot cocoa in my hand, a sweet delight,
As we watch the stars twinkle through the night.

Winter's magic, it's a sight to behold,
A season of stories, waiting to be told.
So let's bundle up and venture outside,
Embracing the wonders that winter provides.

Tanaka Natalie Gundani (14)

A Joyous Occasion

Snowflakes gently fall,
Blanketing the Earth in white,
A warm and joyful Christmas.

Children's laughter rings,
As they build snowmen with glee,
Gifts under the tree.

Fire crackles bright,
Bathing the room in golden light,
Love fills the air.

Families gather,
Sharing meals and stories dear,
Hearts full of cheer.

Carols softly sung.
Voices harmonize as one,
Peace and love embrace.

Candles flicker bright,
Guiding us through the dark night,
Hope shines in our hearts.

A warm and joyful Christmas,
Spreading kindness near and far,
Blessings all around.

Skylar Jolly (11)

The Essence Of Christmas

Winter joy and festive fun,
The apricity of the wakening sun,
Distant carols, chimes of bells,
Cinnamon, clementine, festive smells,
The merry twinkling of each fairy light,
The shining stars of a December night,
Flickering flames of a cosy fire,
A silent night from the local choir,
The excitement as each present is unwrapped,
The laughter as each cracker is pulled
and snapped,
Pigs in blankets, sprouts, gravy and more,
Wrapping paper all over the floor,
Grandparents falling asleep in their chairs,
Children cuddling their new teddy bears,
The generosity, kindness and glee,
That's what Christmas means to me.

Bella Lane (14)

Santa's Magical Night

A mythical delight known as Santa Claus,
Is the story of a guy with a bright heart,
Who lives in a land of snow and dazzling lights,
Where joy fills the air every night.

He crosses the world bringing joy to everyone,
Wearing a tall hat and a crimson coat.
With his sleigh so fast
And his magnificent reindeer pulling it,
He sent gifts to every land.

Let the festivities commence as Santa sends
Pleasure down the chimney with a cheery smile.
His laugh is so joyful
That it spreads warmth like a stinky dish of jelly,
Making his tummy tremble like one.
As the stars come out on Christmas Eve,
Santa Claus is on his way and there will be gifts!

Param Ghelani (7)

Winter

The street cars are like frosted cakes
All covered with cold, icy snowflakes
Looking out the window
Snowing with deep thoughts
Looking at the window
Drinking hot coffee
Outside freezing cold
Making snowmen outside
The families having fun, giving gifts
I look at how happy they are
Snow is fun and joy
Snowball fights
Building stuff with snow
Laughing and smiling with laughter on their faces
Ice skating, buying stuff
Taking pictures with your friends
At night, you see enormous controversial stars
Up in the deep blue sky that sparkles all night
People with loads of love, respect and kindness.

Mansa Tahir (9)

The Day Before Christmas

The wind was blowing, the snow was glowing.
Santa's bag was packed and the presents
were wrapped.
The kids were in bed and Santa was dressed in red.
The sleigh was ready to go, and the reindeer were
all lined up in a row,
With one big flicker of light, Santa was out of sight.

He jumped down the chimneys, giving toys to little
girls and boys.
He munched up cookies
Because only he knows how it feels to eat so
many meals!
After he was done, he was no longer on the run,
So he visited Rome before he went home.
Then he hugged Mrs Claus and received
elven applause.
He took off his reds and went to bed.

Anastazja Clark (9)

Holme House Christmas

The scent of cinnamon sticks fills the air
Presents wrapped neatly with pink silky bows
Twinkling, winking fairy lights make the room glow
Perched on top of the Christmas tree
Is the magnificent Golden Angel fair

Crackling fire is an amazing sight
Orange flames and red coals glowing
Creating long shadows growing
Fingers of flames twisting and flickering
Up the chimney they take flight

Family gather for a delicious dinner
Mountain-high piles of crispy roasts
A magic mix of sangria for the Christmas toast
Tasty turkey snuggled up with pigs in blankets
Warm chocolate pudding is a real winner.

Lily Marsden-Mellin (11)

Eid Is Great

Eid is fun and great,
It is time to celebrate

Eid Mubarak to everyone,
Come on, let's have fun

Everyone is going to the mosque to pray,
People are grateful, it's a special day

"Mmm!" the taste of delicious food,
Really puts you in a good mood.

Everybody is wearing their posh clothes
And the guys are cruising
With their flash cars on the road.

Children opening their gifts with a smile,
And having fun,
Going out to different places.

All of a sudden, the days come to an end,
Well, what can I say?
This is one of my favourite days.

Syeda Bisma (13)

Christmas

C elebrations around the world and majestic moments happen every year,
H eart-warming gatherings and a day where you can never feel fear.
R avishing Christmas trees decorated and filled with love,
I lluminating lights glisten and spotted from above.
S now falls gently down as dancing ballerinas in the starlit sky,
T ime by time, the hours fly!
M agical events happen, particularly that night,
A stonishing dust strangely falls from the sky - so who could have done it?
S anta... the greatest wizard of all because without him this poem wouldn't have been made at all!

Mathey Dezhev (11)

The Other Side

Christmas, oh Christmas, I love you so
In particular, your mistletoe
I love it all, from pudding to tree
But not all are as lucky as me

We open presents and stuff our faces
But few live in a perfect oasis
Many can't afford gifts or dinner
For their budget is so much thinner

We do not consider the other side
So let me take you along for a ride
Some have no tree or decorations
And depend on others' kind donations

As we immerse ourselves in celebrations
Enjoying the warmth with all relations
Amongst the fun and hullabaloo
Try to think of others, not just you.

Claudia Muller (12)

The Winter Wonderland

Christmas time has come
Our wonderful winter wonderland has arrived
We all come together
When it is snowy weather
And sing a carol together

Christmas trees are placed
Ornaments hung
As we all sung
Lots of yummy treats
And plenty of seats
For each and every one of us

We watch a movie
Celebrate traditionally
Laughing and cheering
With lots of merriness

Christmas time has come
The time when we all come together
The snow falls

White like the icing from Christmas cookies
And that's when we know
Christmas is merriness and snow.

Syeda Anisa Mumtaz Nakvi (10)

Without Her

Christmas Day at last,
I dance down the stairs,
Joyful and merry.

But something is missing,
Or rather someone,
From my usual Christmas routine.

No phone call to be made,
No gift or card,
No presence at all.

I am without her,
For the first time,
And yet merriness remains.

Her spirit pushes me to stay this way,
To stay joyful,
To celebrate, even without her.

My soul longs to see her again,
To hear her beautiful voice,
To see her beautiful smile.

I am without her,
For the first time,
And yet merriness remains.

Toby Taylor (16)

North Wind Girl

Flakes, far falling
Down from space
Soft and gentle
On your face

Now the clouds
Begin to grow
Now it's turning
Into snow

It's streaming down
In a tide
Dream and reality
Now collide

Twirling, whirling
It's a storm
Air whipped
And leaves torn

I dance and dance
Spin and twist

Squinting through
The snowy mist

Until...

Flakes, far falling
Down from space
Land soft and gentle
On my face

Dream and reality slide apart...
Who am I?
The North Wind Girl.

Mia Flowerday (10)

If I Was An Elf

I'd like to be an elf who works for Santa Claus.
Maybe I could wear a badge
And be in charge of Christmas laws.
In the workshop, I'd work all day.
There must be enough toys to fill Santa's sleigh.
I'll be checking every race track.
It has to be perfect for Santa's sack.
Every doll's house will need a lick of paint.
I don't want a single complaint.
On Christmas Eve our work is almost done.
Santa says, "Hey! It's time for some fun!"
I think every elf needs a break.
This is the time for Christmas cake.
And now it's time to wave off the reindeer...
We'd better get started for next year!

Gregori Masliakovas (9)

Snow

White like fluffy clouds but bite when you touch them.
But the delicate sculpture of the snowflakes gently dances as I watch them closely through my bedroom window.
Its winter.
Winter, the season of joy
When people celebrate and share the holidays are here, the gifts are near but winter has its own warmth
Winter, the season of hope
When days are short and nights are long, the stars are bright and the moon is full but winter has its own light
Winter, the season of love
When hearts are close and hands are held the fire is cosy and the cocoa is sweet but winter has its own magic.

Sara Abdussalam (16)

Winter Wonderland

In the winter wonderland,
There is a beautiful tree,
It stood alive and free,
It was always good to meet the tree.

In the winter wonderland
A squirrel declared the news
Of a cold moving upon the wonderland
Her name was Winter.

In the winter wonderland
The ground was full of cold,
Crunchy white sand as its abode
No sign of an evergreen tree.

The tree began to shiver.
She began to quiver.
Its sacred leaves down-turning
No sun up high, a burning
And it began
To die

In the winter wonderland
An old tree died.

Esther Mbogol (10)

Winter Is Coming

The leaves have fallen and I can see the bird's nest clearly now,
They need some cover to protect their nest.
I try to help, but they are scared.
I can rather fix it once they are away.

Christmas is all about gifts and surprises.
Here I give, one to the birds I love.

I wish I could add some more layers to the nest.
But the birds are back home sooner.

The rabbit does not want to come out of its hole.
Oh wait, I guess there is also a mole.

I wish they could have some hot chocolate to keep them warm.
To remind them it's Christmas and soon the cold will be gone.

Aadita Keshari (7)

Winter Wonderland

Inside the cabin, was where she sat.
A mug of hot chocolate waiting to be drank.
The warmth of the fire cascaded her.
Like a blanket wrapped around her.

As the moon shone upon the land.
The stars twinkled bright in the dreary night.
The snow lightly fluttered upon the snowy ground.

The noise of children's laughter filled her ears.
As they ran down the street
With a handful of that white, angelic snow.
Waiting to be thrown.

She started to remember her childhood.
Her innocence, her eagerness to learn.
A grin plastered on her face.

Ayesha Siddiqah Ahmed (16)

Winter Wonderland

Powder like snow
As it crunches
Cheeky elves giggle
Warm berry juice
Hot chocolate
Marshmallows topped with
Fluffy whipped cream too
Sleds speeding
Ice forming
Then slowly melting
Frost is nature's diamonds
The reindeer munching
Santa laughing
Children sitting on his lap
Now the ice begins to crack
Winter sun
Low and bright
Dazzles all eyes
Now we don't wait for the dark nights
The sleigh bells jingle
Northern Lights glowing green

Saint Old Nick's magic sparkles
As he creeps down the chimney.

Olivia Rose Blake (11)

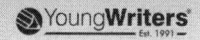

Winter

I love winter, we get to run and play,
Enjoying the snow and celebrating all day!
Snowflakes fall to the ground,
Or into people's open mouths.
Warm and cosy in our residences,
Whilst the wind blows furiously at our canopies.
Hot chocolate and marshmallows are
passed about,
As everyone gathers around the fire in a crowd.

We go out in the snow,
And make snowballs that we can throw!
Or make some dazzling snowmen,
That stay warm with the clothes we put on them.
Although we tremble with the cold,
We brave it because we are bold!
Everyone loves the winter,
We shout and scream as it arrives and cheer!

Azka Bhatti (13)

Santa's Busy Workshop

Elves sprinting all over, checking hurriedly
Fairies swirling around, making clothes fluffy and fuzzy
Trolls carving out unique sculptures from magical wood
Mini engineers mending the sleigh to make sure your gifts are secured

Elves carefully loading the gifts into the sack
With the individual presents filling up the towering racks
Fairies spreading mysterious, glittering powder on the reindeer
As the grand gateway slowly opens clear

Santa commands and they soar through the night sky
Sprinkling magical powder dust as they fly.

Prithviraj Chauhan (11)

A Dark Christmas

Everyone warm's in the light
I freeze in their shadows
Everyone skates on the ice
I trip and fall through
Everyone sings around a beautiful tree
I watch it tower over me
Everyone laughs at their jokes
I hear those who are gone
Everyone is smiling
I get told to smile bright

The darkness of Christmas is a comfortable place to be
Stars are the only light I need
Silence is the best music
The chill is my favourite warmth
The raindrops are the best of friends

Everyone sleeps through the best part of the day
But if they didn't, I don't think it'd be as beautiful.

Alex-Kate Phillips-Hawkes (16)

Winter Sports

Sleighing through blankets of snow,
Gracefully gliding on the ice.
Frosty air with cheeks aglow,
A winter's day that will entice.

Skating softly upon whiteness.
Dancing ecstatically, frosty floor.
Glancing at the sun's brightness,
Prancing sprightly like eagles soar.

Skiing eagerly with fluffy coats,
Swiftly sliding, soft white sheet.
Elegantly drifting as they float,
Passing people, see them greet.

Winter play under snowfall,
Time ticks like swift light.
Fun is had by all,
A wintry joyous sight.

Gisele Yang (9)

New Year

The dark descends around me
Soon will be 2024
The sun will rise and I'll see
Soft, pink dawn

I start to think back
All my jokes and laughs and words
In that whole sky of black
Talking on all those curbs

Then I remembered
A New Year's resolution
And all my friends assembled
And I thought of a solution

"Let's all promise
That with the highs and the lows
Just as we promised
We will always be close!"

And we all leaned in
And repeated as I said

We started to spin
And the pink dawn turned to red

Happy New Year!

Niamh Bacon-Breen (12)

Winter Wonderland

With all the festive food and drinks,
And people skating on ice rinks.
Why don't you come,
To Winter Wonderland with your mum.

The winter will spread with its white sheets,
It surely is the time to greet.
The winter sure is cold,
And that's what makes it so bold.

There is Frosty the Snowman,
And there are penguins with no man.
There is also Buddy the Elf,
He is dancing on the shelf.

Everyone is having fun,
Even one is better than none.
Everyone is with their friends,
Now the fun never ends.

Oshmi Jayakody (11)

Winter Wishes

It's time to make your Christmas list
Full of wants and needs
Oh, Santa's real, Santa exists!
Santa and his reindeer leave
To deliver the toys to all the kids
Across the starry sky, they speed
Santa doesn't like children who tell fibs
All the kids are in their beds
The Christmas lights and decorations too
All over windows and rooftops more
It's such a nice and warming view
When Santa gets in there are cookies, milk and carrots galore
Well, I'll be making my list tonight
Full of happiness and delight.

Alysha Dosanjh (12)

The Icy Grip Of War

'We're on the threshold of winter',
Is a figurative term,
The bone-numbing chill of war,
By its frostbite, they now burn.

For this time the snow is different,
Undergone a change,
It ain't falling on empty fields,
But falling on fresh graves.

No more are the children laughing with joy,
Dancing at winter's delights,
But walking with faces downcast and still,
Futures deprived of light.

For while we laugh, dance and sing,
Lives are in disarray,
People kidnapped and held hostage,
Yet, "They're missing," is what we say.

Tamara Kramer (14)

Winter

Can you see the snow,
And feel the cold.
As we wear our scarves,
Our gloves and coats.
It's winter time,
When the sun doesn't shine,
But it's still beautiful though.

The mystery man comes out to play,
With his many toys in a bag,
It's Christmastime,
Where the elves never hide,
And the best thing you've ever had.

Mister Santa Claus drinks very warm milk,
Throughout the entire day.
He likes cookies and cream,
And he's never mean.
So yet again, let's say!
It's a happy time,
So you better not cry,
And be happy every day.

Purity Ihesie (10)

Teacher, Teacher (Winter Version)

Teacher, teacher,
If you can't find Joe,
He's in the courtyard,
Playing with snow.

Teacher, teacher,
If you can't find Jan,
She's in the playground,
Building a snowman.

Teacher, teacher,
If you can't find Eric,
He's at the gates,
Looking for St. Nick.

Teacher, teacher,
If you can't find Michael,
He's in the library,
Looking for the Bible.

Teacher, teacher,
If you can't find Bree,
She's in the office,
Decorating the tree.

Charmaine Mak (9)

Angel For Alex

As I lay in the snow,
Looking up at the stars,
Making an angel for Alex,
My brother in heaven,
I wonder to myself,
If he can see me,
As I move around,
In the cold crisp snow,
Thinking of him,
On a winter morning,
As I get up,
I look down at the whiteness,
And see his angel,
As I shed a tear,
I know he is near,
As I see a robin in a tree,
When he flew away,
I knew he was happy,
Goodbye, my brother,
I'll see you one day,

But not too near,
As I need to be here...

Daisy Adela Anderson (12)

Where's Your Christmas?

A seed of doubt,
In my mind, an empty field.
Isn't Christmas about joy?
Where's yours?

A shoot of a worry,
For you, are you okay?
Embedding itself into my happiness,
Where's yours?

A growing stump now,
Still thinking, thinking of you.
I get a present every year,
Where's yours?

A towering tree,
I'm trying, trying to save your Christmas.
I have my New Years resolution,
Where's yours?

And it isn't fair,
How your Christmas is bare.

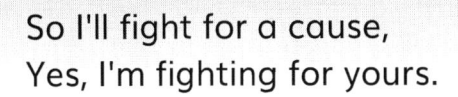

So I'll fight for a cause,
Yes, I'm fighting for yours.

Ellie Bartles-Smith (13)

In The Snowing Wonderland

Winter! Winter! Winter!
Winter is coming soon.

I feel the winter coming for me,
I feel the breeze coming out for me,
I start to freeze outside,
The wind blows me away,
The wind blows me away.

Winter!
Oh, winter!
You're coming out for me,
The snow falls like glitter,
I feel the flakes glimmering down the sky.

Now, it's, not, so, bright, (slow)
It is turning from day to night,
Sun to moon,
Fired to tired,
Now it's time for bed,
In the snowing wonderland!

Halimah Al-Aswad (11)

Solitary Winter Wanderer

The bittersweet shiver of moonlight
Starlight wind bright
The winter enters the breeze of the November nights
The browning piles of once red, once orange leaves
Moulding on the ground long forgotten
The fire warmth and fir tree smell
Christmas smells of cinnamon and fruitcake
The dragon's breath of New Year's Eve
The burst of bright breath held fire sparks
of fireworks
The frost promise of January
The shivers of frost-infused grass
The moon and stars quivering
Twinkling and shifting, sparkling shimmering.

Amy Stevenson (12)

One Small Snowflake

All children awake
All because of,
One small snowflake

Everyone knows
It's winter time
Now let's see this bright time shine,

Gifts brought under the tree
All to see a young child's glee

Now let's settle under the fireplace
And hope to see
That familiar face

Old Saint Nick
With his bag of joy
Holding a bunch
Of special toys.

Now let's all not weep
And go to sleep

And awake in a winter wonderland.
One small snowflake.
Dewi Miles (12)

Winters Whisper: A Christmas Enchantment

In the land of frost, where snowflakes fall
And stars twinkle bright, standing tall
Winter's magic enchants us all
Memories linger within our call.

The fire's warm glow, a comforting sight
While carols echo through the halls at night
Love's embrace, a candle's flickering light
Peace descends as snowflakes take flight.

Beneath the mistletoe, the young hearts sway
Entwined in love, like ivy, all day
Children's laughter brings cheer, come that way
A miracle on this enchanted day.

Olivia Henry (11)

Winter's Queen

Ice glides between her veins,
Now not even a drop of blood remains,
Every tread leaves a chilling bite,
As she slowly subverts the world to white.

Her beauty is so frigid and cold,
Like a story that should never be told,
She has eyes of the bluest hue,
Like a frozen lake that holds the best view.

Her hair looked like chunks of snow,
That cascaded down to the field below,
The locks that once appeared black,
But no more, since the night of the attack.

She is the queen of snow and ice,
If you are thinking of looking, think twice.

Olivia McGregor (16)

Wonderland

I turn to only stare at the blankness outside my window,
A delight... maybe,
If it weren't for the bitterness of the cold
Or the frost forcing you to face numbness,
My breaths impale the window leaving a smoky shape,
Harsh,
Deceptive,
The snow drips and floats down
Landing wherever it pleases,
Covering the suburban land in its power.
It truly is a sight... from a distance,
As are most things,
That is why most people enjoy it,
Embrace it,
For it is our winter wonderland.

Marley Prot-Lane (15)

Snow

The houses are
Like iced cake
All coated and covered up
With snowflakes

The car's tyres
Crunch outside on the street
Their windscreens
Covered with thick sleet

Icicles hang from the buildings,
Gleaming in the light like pure glass.
The silvery lakes are frozen still,
Reflecting the sun above as I walk past.

Trees and bushes are covered with a white coat,
Birds tweeting and flying by.
Snowflakes crash to the ground below,
As the birds look from high in the sky.

Yusuf A Husny (11)

White Christmas

One night in December snow was falling.
Making the ground all fluffy and white.
The children made snowmen
And played in the snow
Making snow angels and sledging down hills.
Once back inside, the children get warm
By a nice cosy fire and a yummy hot drink.
With candy canes and sweets to enjoy with a film.
The house is all decorated with trees and lights
Knowing that Christmas is almost here.
The children search the skies for the reindeer
and Santa
Only a few more nights till Santa arrives.

Lily Turner (8)

Winter Joy

Ice and snow all around
No sunshine to be found
Christmas is coming very soon
We all sing a winter tune

Snow falling everywhere
Some falling in your hair
Some children are playing
Others at home, they are staying

At home cuddling up with a drink
Winter magic comes together in a blink
Christmas trees everywhere
Over here and over there

Winter was so much fun
Very exciting for everyone
Now it's time to say goodbye
Winter will come back another time.

Mawulolo Koliasa (10)

Winter Nights

It is dark out,
The night is eerily frosty.
You would freeze, without a doubt,
The bitter cold can be nasty.
You bundle up to stay warm.

As the piercing wind blows,
You snuggle up, to sleep.
The snowstorm is close,
It starts to creep.

When it's closer everything freezes,
The temperature drops.
Before the wind breaches,
It finally stops.
Coming to an end.

A layer of snow waits,
For the day to come.
It can be seen, on many sites,
Waiting for the grum.

In a matter of moments,
Something is ruined.

Eleanor Lancaster (14)

A One-Of-A-Kind Morning

A blanket of snow covering the grass
Fixed and untouched stretching far and wide,
It blows.
Never a footprint, never a pawprint on the morning snow
Like angels on earth or diamonds shattered in the sky
But none of these describe you just right,
As you are a one-of-a-kind morning.

Through my bedroom window; framed,
As the north winds go
You turn houses into birthday cakes,
And spread pink on our noses.
Smooth, clean, and frosty white
Until we start a snowball fight!

Lara Johnston (9)

Snow, Snow, Snow

December has arrived and Christmas is coming fast.
The nights are getting dark which means it's almost time
Time to write my Christmas list.
Santa, are you ready?
My Christmas list is so long.
Dear Santa, for this Christmas
I want the best thing of all,
I'm sure you know.
I want to have fun like never before.
Santa, I don't want the usual toy bikes or cars.
I want to bring joy to everyone I love.
Dear Santa, all I'm asking for is...
Snow! Snow! Snow!'

Mason James (7)

Winter Wishes

Haikus

In a wonderland
Of the winter season's wish
Our hearts fill with joy

A wonderful time
We are all happy tonight
In winter's true wish

A lovely time
To be all together now
In a wonderland

Full of good wishes
And jolly good Christmas cheer
A winter's true wish

To be happy now
And to never ever frown
For it's a winter's wish

Happy as can be
On this truly wishful night
Of a winter's wish.

Amandeep Bhakar (10)

Winter Dusk Till Dawn

A winter's sky for a winter's morn
Blue ice decorated with clouds
Clouds embroidered with snowflakes
Low-lying sun reaching out-yawning
Bright and burning
Setting light to the horizon
Heavenly glow highlighting Psalm
The horizon wearing its snowy air like a grey quilt
Morning chill dancing with bones
Evening chill dancing the tango
White fairy dust resting on the earth
Decorated with a Christmas hue
Winter morn, Winter dawn
Winter after, Winter dusk.

Holly Hopkinson (14)

Greatest Time Of All

Hang up the stockings,
Decorate the tree,
Presents placed perfectly,
What a delightful sight to see,
Milk and cookies are out,
Kids tucked in bed tight,
There's too much to do!
On Christmas Eve night!
Before you take a snooze,
And dream till the next day,
Don't forget some food,
For the friends that pull the sleigh,
You see reindeer need snacks too,
A little love and fun,
To help Santa through the night,
And get the important job done.

Natalia Winiarska (9)

Encore!

Creeping down the staircase before the first light,
Wondering if she'll find anything or if, perhaps
That last tantrum was one too many.
It never was, of course.

Tearing through the wrapping, laughing,
Singing songs, watching movies by the fire
And eating chocolates galore
Does she even know?

It won't be long now
Before it's just another day.
It came and went this year,
It hardly seemed to stay.

Still, I seem to long,
To long for one last time
Perhaps next year.

Poppy Orr (17)

My Christmas Poem

Winter is here, so Christmas time is near
Snow will be falling then the children will cheer
Santa will be sleighing around this time of year
Delivering presents to those who are dear
Boys and girls all over the world try to sleep
But are waiting to hear the footsteps of reindeer
So they know they are near
Waiting for presents from Santa, the sweet
old dear.

I hope your holidays are full of love and laughter
Be ready for New Year and plenty of days after.

Harley Johnson (6)

Winter Wonderland

Winter Wonderland is so much fun!
C'mon hop onto my reindeer, she's my best one!
Wanna take a ride to the elf workshop?
Just to help you feel like you belong here, why not wear this top?
Wanna give Saint Nic some cookies, he's really hungry
Remember, go out for him with a big lookie!
Good or bad, just come here
Knock on the door with a loud *knock, knock!*
See ya later, it's time to go, oh Saint Nic says, "Ho, ho, ho!"

Zikoranaudodimma Iyayi (8)

On A Christmas Night

Far up in the north,
Auroras glimmered in the jet-black night,
Lighting it up with beauty.
Treetops covered with snow,
Pierced the night with its sharp edges.
On Christmas Night.

Glorious hymns rang through the night.
Bells jingled and the clock tower banged.
Twelve o'clock on the dot.
On Christmas Night.

Soon, Father Christmas would appear.
Presents would be placed under the tree.
Children would squeal in delight.
And then, well, you'd see the beauty
Of Christmas night.

Aizah Nadeem (10)

Christmas

It's Christmas, let's celebrate
With joy, happiness and elate
Presents to every girl and boy
There is delight within every toy.

Presents being given to the poor
This is a holiday that we should all adore
Whether it is fighting with the snow
It is happiness that all should show.

Santa will come
For every daughter and son
With presents in his bay
Riding and riding in his sleigh

Nice list,
Naughty list
You better watch out
You better not be missed.

Ali Fareed (11)

Christmas Wonderland

- **C** hristmas carols
- **H** o, ho, ho!
- **R** udolph
- **I** love Christmas
- **S** now
- **T** ree
- **M** ilk and cookies
- **A** snowball fight
- **S** anta Claus

- **W** inter Wonderland
- **O** rnaments
- **N** o more school
- **D** elicious food
- **E** ating sweets
- **R** eindeer
- **L** ove and care
- **A** lways let it snow
- **N** ativity plays
- **D** ancing the night away.

Betty Rogers (9)

That Time Of Year

There's a breeze in the air,
So we all take care.
As it starts to snow,
We begin to know.
It's that time of year.

Jack Frost has been,
As we all started to dream.
So we all get nice and cosy,
As it gets all stormy.
It's that time of year.

Santa Claus is coming,
So the elves start their Christmas shopping
As we wake up on Christmas Day,
All we do is sit and play.
It's that time of year.

Owen Taylor (12)

As Pure As The Driven Snow

Stargazing into a dark sky,
So empty yet so full of hidden memories.
I call out into the bitter unknown,
My voice is stretched out
And carried like songbirds echoing in the frosty trees,
Vibrating the atmosphere
With a warmth beyond an ethereal spectral.
Only to be perceived by those with hearts so cold,
Like the petals of white roses
Falling to the corrupt ground,
Gracing it with their presence.
As pure as the driven snow.

Ameerah Ghariani (16)

In The Winter

I see the snow-coated forest,
In the winter,
I see the trees glistening in the morning sun,
In the winter,
I think of it like a cupcake with icing sugar on top,
In the winter,
I see that all the puddles and lakes are frozen over,
In the winter,
I hear the crunch of the snow
under my winter boots,
In the winter,
I snuggle up in front of the fire,
In the winter,
I have a hot chocolate in my hands,
In the winter.

Imogen Gannon (12)

I Wonder What Their Christmas Is Like

Do they spend it alone?
Do they have quality time?
Are they surrounded by family and friends, feeling all warm and nice,
Or are they desperate and hoping that they are surrounded by life?
I wish I could say to them that it's going to be alright,
Look through their eyes and see what it's truly like.
Christmas is a time of joy and happiness.
So let it be,
I really wish we could all be merry,
Especially on Christmas Day.

Kacey Compton (13)

My Winter Wonderland

Comes up a morning
With a chill in the air

Oh, what a wonderful sight
With a blanket of snow on the ground
Glistening white

Although the crisp air bites your skin
Nothing can hold the merriment within
Children playing, snowball fights
What's not to do on this winter's night?

It's a Winter Wonderland
There's anything you can do
A whirlwind of possibilities
It's all up to you.

Anaya Hassan (11)

Christmas

C offee-coloured Christmas pudding
H ot chocolate melting in my throat
R oaring fires... *Crackle! Pop! Bang!*
I can smell Santa's smelly socks!
S ee kids singing in the streets
T winkling tinsel wrapped around the Christmas tree like a warm hug
M elting apple pie bubbling in my throat
A peppermint candy cane tingling on your tongue
S nowflakes floating into my mouth.

Samantha Hull (7)

Santa And Rudolph

Christmas is around the corner
Rudolph drags Santa around
Santa slowly crosses the border
He tiptoes across the house with no sound

Santa delivers the presents
The children take with consent
Santa merrily bobs his head around
Giving the festive round of people down

The Christmas lights are so bright
It gives this world a piece of light
But in the end, we realise
Santa is the person who carries our might.

Sancheka Sreeharan (11)

Christmas Season

It's Christmas season
When both the dead and the living
Come together to be happy,
And celebrate God
Who gave them what they curry.

So I spread joy and be merry,
Knowing the jolly fat man is near me.
Who gives me presents,
Just for being pleasant.

So be good all year
'Cause he watches how you spread cheer.
And put a camera outside
'Cause you might see old Rudolph,
With his nose so bright.
And Santa singing Silent Night.

Precious Onuoha (10)

Warm Winter

In the house, by the fire,
You can slightly hear a choir,
As they sing their song,
Lots of others sing along.

In a chair, nice and snug,
With your hands wrapped around a mug,
As you smell, fresh cookies baking,
You can see the Christmas craft your brother is making.

Outside of the window,
Are children playing in the snow,
All excited for Christmas Day,
When they have new games to play.

Paige Polley (9)

Winter Is Here

Winter is here once again
All the animals are sleeping in their dens
A lot of rest they gain
Except the cold-blooded animals like hens

At the crack of dawn
The hens let out a cackle
They run around the lawn
As the fox tries to tackle

The fish in the water look dead
They are not moving at their best
"It's too hard to fish," the fishermen said
The fish feel so blessed.

Meerab Sheikh (13)

Winter Gifts

The winter snow
A fire's glow
Our faces rosy
Our houses cosy

Robins sing
Bells ring
All the world is glittering

Books are read
Kind words said
There's season spirit
And cheer of no limit

Starry nights
Fairy lights
All the world becomes so bright

Frosted grounds
Creature sounds
Candy canes
And crowded lanes

The people are a merry band
Walking hand in hand
Across this winter wonderland.

Tyler James Forth (16)

Christmas

It is snowing
Nights are glowing
The Christmas spirits are really flowing
Rudolph's sleigh
People play
Children are excited and are shouting, "Yay!"
Naughty elves
On decorated shelves
People not caring about themselves
Down below
People bow
As the sky fills with snow
In the sky
Angles say, "Hi!"
This is the end of my poem and I'd like to say bye.

Nathania Chimduwem (8)

Merry Christmas

It's Christmas,
Where is the tree?
Where are the candles?
Where are the socks?
Where are the lights?
Where is the joy?

Santa is here,
Get ready,
Your cookies will finish,
Don't forget about the milk!

The reindeer will fly,
Joy will try,
Everyone will smile,

Merry Christmas,
Christmas is here,
Make it special,
It's only once a year.

Umaima Mukhtar Zia (13)

Snowy Day

W inter is the best
I love it when it snows
N ew snow is perfect for making a friend
T hen I find the hat, gloves, scarf and carrot
E veryone is staying warm by the fire
R ushing into the kitchen to make hot chocolate
T he time has come to get snuggly on the sofa
I n a warm and fluffy blanket
M um reads us a story
E very night before bed.

Sophie Goodier (11)

One Winter's Day

Winter is here!
Time to have some fun.

Snowballs here and snowballs there,
Up in the air and down below.

Time to have some fun!
Footprints leading to my toes.
Time to be a snow angel!

The evening has arrived.
Time to pack away.
Inside we go with a...

Nice warm fire,
And a hot cup of tea,
And on the couch, all snuggled up.
Ready for some telly.

Haiqa Aziz (9)

Winter Miracle

Christmas is a happy time of year,
But last year it wasn't for me,
Mommy was poorly and nearly died,
But she fought so hard and stayed alive,
This year will be different
and will be magical you'll see,
It isn't about presents or having new toys,
It's about having your loved ones around,
That one day will no longer be here,
And that's what Christmas means to me.

Keelan Stringer (9)

My Christmas Acrostic Poem

- **C** himing of the bell in the church
- **H** appy people and festive cheers
- **R** ising star from all above
- **I** lluminated houses celebrating the good time
- **S** teaming turkey on a plate
- **T** rying to wait for the Christmas delight
- **M** aking the children happy with their exciting gifts
- **A** lways bringing joy to us
- **S** houting sounds of happiness and joy!

Victoria Anyaegbu (9)

The Elf

The elf on the shelf
Was sat by himself.
He was so lonely
He moved very slowly.

He has no friends
So into the wall, he blends.
He wants to be noticed
And have a friend who was closest.

A package arrived
And his spirits revived.
He opened it gladly
And found an elf called Bradley.

They formed a quick bond
And sunglasses were donned.
They went to the beach
And made a sandcastle each.

Ella Koc (8)

Christmas

C hristmas is a wonderful time of the year
H aving fun and bringing good cheer
R ain and snow pour very wet
I mages in heads are always met
S anta riding in his sleigh
T eardrops roll down day after day
M agnificent meals are called delicious
A nd elves are called ridiculous
S haring Christmas stories and saying goodbye.

Isabella Howes-Warnes (10)

I Think About A Christmas

I dream about a winter,
A winter with lots of snow,
With presents under the tree,
Stacked row on row.

Lights, cheers and carols,
Made for all the years,
Never shall one shed a tear,
Never shall one live in fear,
For the goal of Christmas,
Is happiness and joy,
And socks full of toys.

Christmas is for everyone,
Whether young or old,
Where stories get told,
The mystery of Christmas unfolds.

Amaoge Okoli (15)

Winter

W ow, this doesn't seem real. The air is so crisp and fresh.
I take a deep breath and allow the air to enter my flesh.
N ever again will I underestimate the power of air.
T o be honest, I can't do it anyway. It's everywhere.
E xcept whenever winter comes along cold and dark.
R ealisation hits that maybe I can start a little spark.

Rifky Izaak (15)

A Christmas Time

Around midnight, I get a present
Though I didn't fight, it never got a dent
Dreaming and thinking about the ice
Caring and blinking on time

He would say, "Ho, ho, ho!"
But then fades away in the sleigh
With empty plates on the ground

The next morning, I got up
With joy on my face
Unwrapping the presents
It is Christmas time!

Kabiven Vivekanantharajah (11)

Just Enough To Share The Joy

Fir trees dressed in baubles,
Just enough to fit all the presents under.
Crackers big and wide,
Just enough to pull for a sibling or two.
Hot cocoa swirls in a cup,
Just enough to share with the whole family.
Singing Christmas carols,
Just enough to share the joy and love.
When opening the presents,
I saw a card that said:
'Enjoy the joy of Christmas,
Not the presents but the love'.

Adele Amour (10)

A Winter's Day

On a winter's day,
In a land far away,
A star shines bright,
In the lonely night,

A ghostly angel
Appears in that night
And tells the shepherds to quickly take flight,
To Bethlehem where a baby is born.

So in the dead of night,
When the shepherds take flight,
They find the baby,
And think that maybe,
They know who he is...

Catherine Holmes (9)

Land Of Snow

Dancing in the sky
Falling onto the green, green grass
Bright white like a vibrant light.
Glistening in the moonlight.

Cold but soothing, soft like a blanket.
Snow is an extraordinary thing
Sometimes it can have a bit of bling.

Its beauty is majestic.
The way it feels, moves and looks
It's the only thing keeping the snowmen alive.

Kadie Rasmussen (16)

The Wonderland

The trees are icy,
And the branches are snowy,
Footsteps in the snow,
Going too far for you to know.
Children building glistening snowmen,
On the frosty mornings and chilly nights,
Cosy fires and warm holiday delights
Oh, beautiful wonderland,
Where have the times gone?
Where the snowflakes danced,
And the air was crisp looking so white.

Ashleen Khela (11)

The Beauty Of Winter

By the fireplace, a cat curled,
Then outside the winter wind swirled.
I put on my gloves, coat, and scarf,
And walk on the frozen path.
All I see are blankets of snow,
Looking at the moon shimmer and glow.
Trees and grass turning white,
I look at the stars in the winter night.
Every morning I open my door,
Hearing choirs sing more and more.

Arabella Pasquariello (9)

Going December

Air freezes
leaves go soggy and crisp
pavement glitter resumes
in the morning, the sky is made of wisps
in the afternoon, it reverses back to the
cold darkness
giant snowflake illuminating
puddle becomes pavement
cold bells toll
I see my breath before my teeth clack,
the new songbirds so dark so soon;
though a new year arises.

E R Harper (16)

The Most Wonderful Time Of The Year

W hen the glistening snow is falling down
I nside the house is safe and sound
N ice Santa is sending gifts to those favourite boys and girls
T he elves are dancing in the air with magical twirls
E ach family is celebrating with love and laughters
R inging bells tell everyone that Christmas time is here.

Noelle Ngan (7)

The Hibernation

When it's winter
I feel bad
Because when I don't see any animals
I feel really sad.
I'm not sure if you have heard,
But in winter, animals hibernate
Like hedgehogs, dormice, squirrels and birds.
I like animals playing together,
That is what makes me cheerful.
When animals hibernate, I am tearful.

Samuel Kiwanuka-Musoke (7)

Winter's Tale

Winter rushed though
The whispering forest
Icicles down his throat
Crunching leaves and branches
Until there is no more to be found

Winter flattened the bumpy grounds
And took the leaves away
But all of a sudden
I question myself, is that how Winter was made?
But as soon as that, Winter was away.

Amrit Singh Pannu (8)

Christmas Time

It is here, Christmas time
Now the bells will chime and chime
It is near winter time
Shut your doors, it's Christmas time
Santa's coming to hand out love and cheer
This is my favourite time of year
Winter time gets cold and snows
Will it be a white Christmas?
Nobody knows.

Ariana Jones (8)

Christmas Eve

It's Christmas Eve and the stars glow
The only thing to be heard is a ho, ho, ho
It's feeling very merry
But the cold is getting heavy
Santa's riding on his sleigh
Bringing presents, yes he may
Christmas morning
Mum and Dad are yawning
Love and laughter fill the air.

Blossom Huntington (8)

Snowman

Snowman, snowman
Round and white
I wonder what you do at night

Snowman, snowman
Let's have fun before you melt
In the warm spring sun
It is winter, I saw some snow on the cars
My snowman was covered in snow
When I went outside
I made him a new friend.

Mia Spilsbury (8)

Christmas Is Here

I inhale the calming scent of gingerbread,
Of cinnamon,
Of hot chocolate,
I smile as I gaze upon the snow-filled sky,
Upon the fairy lights,
Upon the bright baubles,
I relax as I feel the pine needles,
The fluffy snow,
The wrapped presents,
Christmas is here.

Chloe Griffiths (12)

Winter Wonderland Poems

W onderful winter is here,
I n my garden, there are piles of snow,
N ow I can make a snowman,
T he trees are white with snow,
E verything is covered in sparkly frost,
R ight until we drink hot chocolate with marshmallows!

Esha Raheel (10)

The Winter Feast

The cold night
The cold sky
The cold breeze

There was only that one true Christmas night
There is only that one meal for you
There is only that one true family for you too

One merry Christmas
Two wonderful meals
Three wise men.

Charlie Page (13)

Evergreen

Evergreen, Evergreen, oh so green
Evergreen, Evergreen, soon to be seen
Evergreen, Evergreen, Christmas is near
Evergreen, Evergreen, up every year
Evergreen, Evergreen, a special kind of tree
Evergreen, Evergreen, presents under for you and me.

Chester Steele (7)

Winter Fun

Winter is a time of giving and receiving.
Have some fun and keep on breathing.
Don't let your treats go to waste.
You will lose your taste.
Don't forget to give some love
And enjoy the time with your family!

Daisy Corbet (13)

Christmas Night

Red, green, blue
Gold and white
Fun lights
Tree is bright
Snow-white
Letters to write
For Santa's prize
In red and white
Santa Claus arrived
On Christmas night
Ho, ho, ho!

Sayara Munasinghe (5)

Snow

S oftly falls the blanket of white
N estling upon the Earth in pure delight
O ver hills and fields, a tranquil delight
W hispering tales of a serene night.

Dhruvi Patel (9)

Santa

S ound on the roof
A noise like a hoof
N o cookies or milk
T ons of teddies soft like silk
A voice that goes, "Ho, ho, ho!"

Carly-Jade Sharman (12)

Fun At Winter Wonderland

Diamanté poem

Winter Wonderland
Fun, happy
Eating, laughing, playing
Hot dogs, churros, rollercoaster, fun house
Spinning, shouting, throwing
Fast, scary
Rides.

Logan Esposito Dotchin (7)

Winter Wish

Every winter I wish for snow,
But every year it's always a no.
Every time I look out my window
There's never any snow so I say, "Ohhhh!"

Mia Drummond (9)

Winter's Frosty

The winter's frosty
But not trusty.
I'm colder than ice
But longer than a line.
I'm much rainier
But not like summer.
My weather is frosty
But not roasty.

Janiru Kudahetty (9)

Young Writers Information

We hope you have enjoyed reading this book – and that you will continue to in the coming years.

If you're the parent or family member of an enthusiastic poet or story writer, do visit our website **www.youngwriters.co.uk/subscribe** and sign up to receive news, competitions, writing challenges and tips, activities and much, much more! There's lots to keep budding writers motivated!

If you would like to order further copies of this book, or any of our other titles, then please give us a call or order via your online account.

Young Writers
Remus House
Coltsfoot Drive
Peterborough
PE2 9BF
(01733) 890066
info@youngwriters.co.uk

Join in the conversation!
Tips, news, giveaways and much more!

YoungWritersUK YoungWritersCW
youngwriterscw youngwriterscw